Careers in Focus

FILM

WITHDRAWN

Ferguson

An imprint of Infobase Publishing

Careers in Focus: Film

Ferguson
An imprint of Infobase Publishing
132 West 31st Street
New York NY 10001

Library of Congress Cataloging-in-Publication Data
Careers in focus. Film.
    p. cm.
    Includes index.
    ISBN 0-8160-6561-6   (hc: alk. paper)
    1. Motion pictures—Vocational guidance. I. J.G. Ferguson Publishing
Company.
    PN1995.9.P75C37 2006
    791.43023—dc22   2005026259

Ferguson books are available at special discounts when purchased in bulk quantities for businesses, associations, institutions, or sales promotions. Please call our Special Sales Department in New York at (212) 967-8800 or (800) 322-8755.

You can find Ferguson on the World Wide Web at http://www.fergpubco.com

Text design by David Strelecky

Printed in the United States of America

MP JT 10 9 8 7 6 5 4 3

This book is printed on acid-free paper.

Table of Contents

Introduction

The film industry holds a place in the American imagination like no other, while also maintaining a firm hold on the American pocketbook. The U.S. moviegoing public spends approximately $8 billion annually at the box office. We rent and purchase our favorite films on video and DVD and subscribe to many cable channels devoted to the 24-hour repeats of recent and classic productions. We read magazines and books about filmmaking and visit Web pages devoted to our favorite stars and movies. And thousands of people flock to Hollywood every year to invest in a more glamorous life, with dreams of becoming an actor, screenwriter, or director.

Careers in Focus: Film describes a variety of careers in this glamorous, yet highly competitive, industry—on movie sets that range from Hollywood soundstages, to the windswept deserts of Tunisia, to the packed city streets in Tokyo; in animation, production, and recording studios; in business offices; and in countless other settings. There are film careers for creative people who like to be the center of attention (actors and stunt performers); people who are creative, but like to work behind the scenes (art directors, costume designers, cinematographers, composers and arrangers, screenwriters, and special effects technicians); people with business acumen (producers and talent agents and scouts); and people who enjoy the more technical aspects of the industry (audio recording engineers and lighting technicians).

Although formal education is available for most careers in the film industry, creativity, talent, ambition, perseverance, and "knowing the right people" are often the true keys to making or breaking a career in this highly competitive industry.

Salaries can range from nearly nonexistent for struggling actors to millions of dollars for well-known directors, producers, actors, and others in the industry.

The U.S. Department of Labor predicts that employment in the arts, entertainment, and recreation industries will grow faster than the average through 2012. Experts predict that big budget films will likely continue to rule the industry. Production companies will hire the most popular big-name actors and directors to draw huge profits. Special effects and animation will continue to create new jobs for those talented with computers. Computer-generated imagery is being used increasingly on all films, not just science fiction and horror projects; filmmakers use computers to create crowd scenes, detailed backdrops, and other elements common in films.

1

Today, movie production is inseparable from the TV and video industries. Companies make films to be released in theaters, but also plan for future video rentals and sales and TV showings. Feature films are more frequently produced specifically for release on TV, both network and cable, and then are produced on video.

Constantly changing TV and video technologies both challenge and feed the film industry. DVD, for example, offers viewers much more than a theater experience with the inclusion of director's cuts, outtakes, and commentary on the making of the film. Viewers can skip to their favorite parts of a movie, watch it in a different language, or choose from various formats. HDTV offers such high quality picture that some people say it is better than seeing a movie in a theater. Although HDTV proponents predict that the new TVs will have a serious effect on box office receipts, the technology is still cost-prohibitive for most Americans. As it becomes more affordable, there may be a change in the habits of moviegoers similar to what happened in the 1950s with the introduction of black-and-white TV, but it is likely that the film and television industries will continue to challenge each other and enjoy a competitive coexistence.

Each article in this book discusses a particular film occupation in detail. The articles in *Careers in Focus: Film* appear in Ferguson's *Encyclopedia of Careers and Vocational Guidance,* but have been updated and revised with the latest information from the U.S. Department of Labor, professional organizations, and other sources. The following paragraphs detail the sections and features that appear in the book.

The **Quick Facts** section provides a brief summary of the career including recommended school subjects, personal skills, work environment, minimum educational requirements, salary ranges, certification or licensing requirements, and employment outlook. This section also provides acronyms and identification numbers for the following government classification indexes: the *Dictionary of Occupational Titles* (DOT), the *Guide for Occupational Exploration* (GOE), the National Occupational Classification (NOC) Index, and the Occupational Information Network (O*NET)-Standard Occupational Classification System (SOC) index. The DOT, GOE, and O*NET-SOC indexes have been created by the U.S. government; the NOC index is Canada's career-classification system. Readers can use the identification numbers listed in the Quick Facts section to access further information about a career. Print editions of the DOT (*Dictionary of Occupational Titles.* Indianapolis, Ind.: JIST Works, 1991) and GOE (*Guide for Occupational Exploration.* 3d ed. Indianapolis, Ind.: JIST Works, 2001) are available at libraries.

Electronic versions of the NOC (http://www23.hrdc-drhc.gc.ca) and O*NET-SOC (http://online.onetcenter.org) are available on the World Wide Web. When no DOT, GOE, NOC, or O*NET-SOC numbers are present, this means that the U.S. Department of Labor or Human Resources Development Canada have not created a numerical designation for this career. In this instance, you will see the acronym "N/A," or not available.

The **Overview** section is a brief introductory description of the duties and responsibilities involved in this career. Oftentimes, a career may have a variety of job titles. When this is the case, alternative career titles are presented.

The **History** section describes the history of the particular job as it relates to the overall development of its industry or field.

The Job describes the primary and secondary duties of the job.

Requirements discusses high school and postsecondary education and training requirements, any certification or licensing that is necessary, and other personal requirements for success in the job.

Exploring offers suggestions on how to gain experience in or knowledge of the particular job before making a firm educational and financial commitment. The focus is on what can be done while still in high school (or in the early years of college) to gain a better understanding of the job.

The **Employers** section gives an overview of typical places of employment for the job.

Starting Out discusses the best ways to land that first job, be it through the college placement office, newspaper ads, or personal contact.

The **Advancement** section describes what kind of career path to expect from the job and how to get there.

Earnings lists salary ranges and describes the typical fringe benefits.

The **Work Environment** section describes the typical surroundings and conditions of employment—whether indoors or outdoors, noisy or quiet, social or independent. Also discussed are typical hours worked, any seasonal fluctuations, and the stresses and strains of the job.

The **Outlook** section summarizes the job in terms of the general economy and industry projections. For the most part, outlook information is obtained from the U.S. Bureau of Labor Statistics and is supplemented by information taken from professional associations. Job growth terms follow those used in the *Occupational Outlook Handbook*. Growth described as "much faster than the average" means an increase of 36 percent or more. Growth described as "faster than the average" means an increase of 21 to 35 percent. Growth described as "about as fast as the average" means an increase of 10 to 20 percent. Growth described as "more slowly than the average" means an increase of 3 to 9 percent. Growth described as "little or no change" means an increase of 0 to 2 percent. "Decline" means a decrease of 1 percent or more.

Each article ends with **For More Information,** which lists organizations that provide information on training, education, internships, scholarships, and job placement.

Careers in Focus: Film also includes photos, informative sidebars, and interviews with professionals in the field.

Actors

OVERVIEW

Actors play parts or roles in dramatic productions on the stage, in motion pictures, or on television or radio. They impersonate, or portray, characters by speech, gesture, song, and dance. There are approximately 139,000 actors working in the United States.

HISTORY

Drama, which began as a component of religious festivals, was refined as an art form by the ancient Greeks, who used the stage as a forum for topical themes and stories. The role of actors became more important than in the past, and settings became more realistic with the use of scenery. Playgoing was often a great celebration, a tradition carried on by the Romans. The rise of the Christian church put an end to theater in the sixth century A.D., and for several centuries actors were ostracized from society, surviving as jugglers and jesters.

Drama was reintroduced during the Middle Ages but became more religious in focus. Plays during this period typically centered around biblical themes, and roles were played by craftspeople and other amateurs. This changed with the rediscovery of Greek and Roman plays in the Renaissance. Professional actors and acting troupes toured the countries of Europe, presenting ancient plays or improvising new dramas based on cultural issues and situations of the day. Actors began to take on more prominence in society. In England, actors such as Will Kemp and Richard Burbage became known for their roles in the plays of William Shakespeare. In France, Molière wrote and often acted in his own plays. Until the mid-17th century, however, women were banned from the stage, and young boys played the roles of women.

QUICK FACTS

School Subjects
English
Theater/dance

Personal Skills
Artistic
Communication/ideas

Work Environment
Indoors and outdoors
Primarily multiple locations

Minimum Education Level
High school diploma

Salary Range
$13,790 to $23,462 to $117,478+

Certification or Licensing
None available

Outlook
About as fast as the average

DOT
150

GOE
01.05.01

NOC
5135

O*NET-SOC
27-2011.00

By the 18th century, actors could become quite prominent members of society, and plays were often written—or, in the case of Shakespeare's plays, rewritten—to suit a particular actor. Acting styles tended to be highly exaggerated, with elaborate gestures and artificial speech, until David Garrick introduced a more natural style to the stage in the mid-1700s. The first American acting company was established in Williamsburg, Virginia, in 1752, led by Lewis Hallan. In the next century, many actors became stars: famous actors of the time included Edwin Forrest, Fanny and Charles Kemble, Edmund Kean, William Charles Macready, and Joseph Jefferson, who was particularly well known for his comedic roles.

Until the late 19th century, stars dominated the stage. But in 1874, George II, Duke of Saxe-Meiningen, formed a theater troupe in which every actor was given equal prominence. This ensemble style influenced others, such as Andre Antoine of France, and gave rise to a new trend in theater called naturalism, which featured far more realistic characters in more realistic settings than before. This style of theater came to dominate the 20th century. It also called for new methods of acting. Konstantin Stanislavsky of the Moscow Art Theater, who developed an especially influential acting style that was later called method acting, influenced the Group Theater in the United States; one member, Lee Strasberg, founded The Actors Studio in New York, which would become an important training ground for many of the great American actors. In the early 20th century, vaudeville and burlesque shows were extremely popular and became the training ground for some of the great comic actors of the century.

By then, developments such as film, radio, and television offered many more acting opportunities than ever before. Many actors honed their skills on the stage and then entered one of these new media, where they could become known throughout the nation and often throughout the world. Both radio and television offered still more acting opportunities in advertisements. The development of sound in film caused many popular actors from the silent era to fade from view, while giving rise to many others. But almost from the beginning, film stars were known for their outrageous salaries and lavish style of living.

In the United States, New York gradually became the center of theater and remains so, although community theater companies abound throughout the country. Hollywood is the recognized center of the motion picture and television industries. Other major production centers are Miami, Chicago, San Francisco, and Austin.

THE JOB

The imitation or basic development of a character for presentation to an audience often seems like a glamorous and fairly easy job. In reality, it is demanding, tiring work requiring a special talent.

The actor must first find a part available in some upcoming production. This may be in a comedy, drama, musical, or opera. Then, having read and studied the part, the actor must audition before the director and other people who have control of the production. This requirement is often waived for established artists. In film and television, actors must also complete screen tests, which are scenes recorded on film, at times performed with other actors, which are later viewed by the director and producer of the film.

If selected for the part, the actor must spend hundreds of hours in rehearsal and must memorize many lines and cues. This is especially true in live theater; in film and television, actors may spend less time in rehearsal and sometimes improvise their lines before the camera, often performing several attempts, or "takes," before the director is satisfied. Television actors often take advantage of TelePrompTers, which scroll their lines on a screen in front of them while performing. Radio actors generally read from a script, and therefore rehearsal times are usually shorter.

In addition to such mechanical duties, the actor must determine the essence of the character being portrayed and the relation of that character to the overall scheme of the play. Radio actors must be especially skilled in expressing character and emotion through voice alone. In many film and theater roles, actors must also sing and dance and spend additional time rehearsing songs and perfecting the choreography. Some roles require actors to perform various stunts, which can be quite dangerous. Most often, these stunts are performed by specially trained *stunt performers*. Others work as *stand-ins* or *body doubles*. These actors are chosen for specific features and appear on film in place of the lead actor; this is often the case in films requiring nude or seminude scenes. Many television programs, such as game shows, also feature *models*, who generally assist the host of the program.

Actors in the theater may perform the same part many times a week for weeks, months, and sometimes years. This allows them to develop the role, but it can also become tedious. Actors in films may spend several weeks involved in a production, which often takes place on location, that is, in different parts of the world. Television actors involved in a series, such as a soap opera or a situation comedy, also may play the same role for years, generally in 13-week cycles. For these actors, however, their lines change from week to

Actors Uma Thurman and Ben Affleck discuss a scene with director John Woo (center) during a break in filming of the sci-fi thriller *Paycheck*. *(Doug Curran/Paramount/ZUMA/Corbis)*

week and even from day to day, and much time is spent rehearsing their new lines.

While studying and perfecting their craft, many actors work as *extras*, the nonspeaking characters who appear in the background on screen or stage. Many actors also continue their training. A great deal of an actor's time is spent attending auditions.

REQUIREMENTS

High School
There are no minimum educational requirements to become an actor. However, at least a high school diploma is recommended.

Postsecondary Training
As acting becomes more and more involved with the various facets of our society, a college degree will become more important to those who hope to have an acting career. It is assumed that the actor who has completed a liberal arts program is more capable of understanding the wide variety of roles that are available. Therefore, it is strongly recommended that aspiring actors complete at least a bachelor's degree program in theater or the dramatic arts. In addition, graduate degrees in the fine arts or in drama are nearly always required should the individual decide to teach dramatic arts.

College can also provide acting experience for the hopeful actor. More than 500 colleges and universities throughout the country offer dramatic arts programs and present theatrical performances. Actors and directors recommend that those interested in acting gain as much experience as possible through acting in plays in high school and college or in those offered by community groups. Training beyond college is recommended, especially for actors interested in entering the theater. Joining acting workshops, such as The Actors Studio, can often be highly competitive.

Other Requirements

Prospective actors will be required not only to have a great talent for acting but also a great determination to succeed in the theater and motion pictures. They must be able to memorize hundreds of lines and should have a good speaking voice. The ability to sing and dance is important for increasing the opportunities for the young actor. Almost all actors, even the biggest stars, are required to audition for a part before they receive the role. In film and television, they will generally complete screen tests to see how they will appear on film. In all fields of acting, a love for acting is a must. It might take many years for an actor to achieve any success, if at all.

Performers on the Broadway stages must be members of the Actors' Equity Association before being cast. While union membership may not always be required, many actors find it advantageous to belong to a union that covers their particular field of performing arts. These organizations include the Actors' Equity Association (stage), Screen Actors Guild (motion pictures and television films), or American Federation of Television and Radio Artists (TV, recording, and radio). In addition, some actors may benefit from membership in the American Guild of Variety Artists (nightclubs, and so on), American Guild of Musical Artists (opera and ballet), or organizations such as the Hebrew Actors Union or the Guild of Italian American Actors for productions in those languages.

EXPLORING

The best way to explore this career is to participate in school or local theater productions. Even working on the props or lighting crew will provide insight into the field.

Also, attend as many dramatic productions as possible and try to talk with people who either are currently in the theater or have been at one time. They can offer advice to individuals interested in a career in the theater.

Many books have been written about acting, not only concerning how to perform but also about the nature of the work, its offerings, advantages, and disadvantages.

EMPLOYERS

Motion pictures, television, and the stage are the largest fields of employment for actors, with television commercials representing as much as 60 percent of all acting jobs. Most of the opportunities for employment in these fields are either in Los Angeles or in New York. On stage, even the road shows often have their beginning in New York, with the selection of actors conducted there along with rehearsals. However, nearly every city and most communities present local and regional theater productions.

As cable television networks continue to produce more and more of their own programs and films, they will become a major provider of employment for actors. Home video will also continue to create new acting jobs, as will the music video business.

The lowest numbers of actors are employed for stage work. In addition to Broadway shows and regional theater, there are employment opportunities for stage actors in summer stock, at resorts, and on cruise ships.

STARTING OUT

Probably the best way to enter acting is to start with high school, local, or college productions and to gain as much experience as possible on that level. Very rarely is an inexperienced actor given an opportunity to perform on stage or in film in New York or Hollywood. The field is extremely difficult to enter; the more experience and ability beginners have, however, the greater the possibilities for entrance.

Those venturing to New York or Hollywood are encouraged first to have enough money to support themselves during the long waiting and searching period normally required before a job is found. Most will list themselves with a casting agency that will help them find a part as an extra or a bit player, either in theater or film. These agencies keep names on file along with photographs and a description of the individual's features and experience, and if a part comes along that may be suitable, they contact that person. Very often, however, names are added to their lists only when the number of people in a particular physical category is low. For instance, the agency may not have enough athletic young women on their roster, and if the applicant happens to fit this description, her name is added.

To learn more about breaking into this career, you might also consider visiting the Screen Actors Guild's website (http://www.sag.org) to read the online publication *Getting Started as an Actor.*

ADVANCEMENT

New actors will normally start in bit parts and will have only a few lines to speak, if any. The normal procession of advancement would then lead to larger supporting roles and then, in the case of theater, possibly to a role as understudy for one of the main actors. The understudy usually has an opportunity to fill in should the main actor be unable to give a performance. Many film and television actors get their start in commercials or by appearing in government and commercially sponsored public service announcements, films, and programs. Other actors join the afternoon soap operas and continue on to evening programs. Many actors have also gotten their start in on-camera roles such as presenting the weather segment of a local news program. Once an actor has gained experience, he or she may go on to play stronger supporting roles or even leading roles in stage, television, or film productions. From there, an actor may go on to stardom. Only a very small number of actors ever reach that pinnacle, however.

Some actors eventually go into other, related occupations and become drama coaches, drama teachers, producers, stage directors, motion picture directors, television directors, radio directors, stage managers, casting directors, or artist and repertoire managers. Others may combine one or more of these functions while continuing their career as an actor.

EARNINGS

The wage scale for actors is largely controlled through bargaining agreements reached by various unions in negotiations with producers. These agreements normally control the minimum salaries, hours of work permitted per week, and other conditions of employment. In addition, each artist enters into a separate contract that may provide for higher salaries.

In 2005, the minimum daily salary of any member of the Screen Actors Guild (SAG) in a speaking role was $716 or $2,483 for a five-day workweek. Motion picture actors may also receive additional payments known as residuals as part of their guaranteed salary. Many motion picture actors receive residuals whenever films, TV shows, and TV commercials in which they appear are rerun, sold for TV exhibition, or put on videocassette or DVD. Residuals often exceed the actors' original salary and account for about one-third of all actors' income.

A wide range of earnings can be seen when reviewing the Actors' Equity Association's *Annual Report 2003,* which includes a breakdown of average weekly salaries by contract type and location. According to the report, for example, those in "Off Broadway" productions earned an average weekly salary of $700 during the 2002–03 season. Other average weekly earnings for the same period include: San Francisco Bay area theater, $318; New England area theater, $294; Disney World in Orlando, Florida, $683; and Chicago area theater, $487. The report concludes that the median weekly salary for all contract areas is $487. Most actors do not work 52 weeks per year; in fact, the report notes that the 39,981 Equity members in good standing only worked an average 16.4 weeks during the 2002–03 season, with median earnings of $6,418.

According to the U.S. Department of Labor, the median yearly earnings of all actors was $23,462 in 2004. The department also reported the lowest paid 10 percent earned less than $13,790 annually, while the highest paid 10 percent made more than $117,478.

The annual earnings of persons in television and movies are affected by frequent periods of unemployment. Unions offer health, welfare, and pension funds for members working over a set number of weeks a year. Some actors are eligible for paid vacation and sick time, depending on the work contract.

In all fields, well-known actors have salary rates above the minimums, and the salaries of the few top stars are many times higher. Actors in television series may earn tens of thousands of dollars per week, while a few may earn as much as $1 million or more per week. Salaries for these actors vary considerably and are negotiated individually. In film, top stars may earn as much as $20 million per film, and, after receiving a percentage of the gross earned by the film, these stars can earn far, far more.

Until recent years, female film stars tended to earn lower salaries than their male counterparts; the emergence of stars such as Julia Roberts, Jodie Foster, Halle Berry, and others has started to reverse that trend. The average annual earnings for all motion picture actors, however, are usually low for all but the best-known performers because of the periods of unemployment.

WORK ENVIRONMENT

Actors work under varying conditions. Those employed in motion pictures may work in air-conditioned studios one week and be on location in a hot desert the next.

Those in stage productions perform under all types of conditions. The number of hours employed per day or week vary, as do the number of weeks employed per year. Stage actors normally perform eight shows per week with any additional performances paid for as overtime. The basic workweek after the show opens is about 36 hours unless major changes in the play are needed. The number of hours worked per week is considerably more before the opening, because of rehearsals. Evening work is a natural part of a stage actor's life. Rehearsals often are held at night and over holidays and weekends. If the play goes on the road, much traveling will be involved.

A number of actors cannot receive unemployment compensation when they are waiting for their next part, primarily because they have not worked enough to meet the minimum eligibility requirements for compensation. Sick leaves and paid vacations are not usually available to the actor. However, union actors who earn the minimum qualifications now receive full medical and health insurance under all the actors' unions. Those who earn health plan benefits for 10 years become eligible for a pension upon retirement. The acting field is very uncertain. Aspirants never know whether they will be able to get into the profession, and, once in, there are uncertainties as to whether the show will be well received and, if not, whether the actors' talent can survive a bad show.

OUTLOOK

Employment in acting is expected to grow about as fast as the average through 2012, according to the U.S. Department of Labor. There are a number of reasons for this. The growth of satellite and cable television in the past decade has created a demand for more actors, especially as the cable networks produce more and more of their own programs and films. The rise of home video has also created new acting jobs, as more and more films are made strictly for the home video market. Many resorts built in the 1980s and 1990s present their own theatrical productions, providing more job opportunities for actors. Jobs in theater, however, face pressure as the cost of mounting a production rises and as many nonprofit and smaller theaters lose their funding.

Despite the growth in opportunities, there are many more actors than there are roles, and this is likely to remain true for years to come. This is true in all areas of the arts, including radio, television, motion pictures, and theater, and even those who are employed are normally employed during only a small portion of the year. Many actors must supplement their income by working at other jobs, such as secretaries, waiters, or taxi drivers, for example. Almost all performers are members of more than one union in order to take advantage of various opportunities as they become available.

It should be recognized that of the 139,000 or so actors in the United States today, only a small percentage are working as actors at any one time. Of these, few are able to support themselves on their earnings from acting, and fewer still will ever achieve stardom. Most actors work for many years before becoming known, and most of these do not rise above supporting roles. The vast majority of actors, meanwhile, are still looking for the right break. There are many more applicants in all areas than there are positions. As with most careers in the arts, people enter this career out of a love and desire for acting.

FOR MORE INFORMATION

The following is a professional union for actors in theater and "live" industrial productions, stage managers, some directors, and choreographers.

Actors' Equity Association
165 West 46th Street
New York, NY 10036
Tel: 212-869-8530
Email: info@actorsequity.org
http://www.actorsequity.org

This union represents television and radio performers, including actors, announcers, dancers, disc jockeys, newspersons, singers, specialty acts, sportscasters, and stuntpersons.

American Federation of Television and Radio Artists
260 Madison Avenue
New York, NY 10016-2402
Tel: 212-532-0800
Email: aftra@aftra.com
http://www.aftra.com

A directory of theatrical programs may be purchased from NAST. For answers to a number of frequently asked questions concerning education, visit the NAST website.

National Association of Schools of Theater (NAST)
11250 Roger Bacon Drive, Suite 21
Reston, VA 20190-5248
Tel: 703-437-0700
Email: info@arts-accredit.org
http://nast.arts-accredit.org/index.jsp

The following union provides general information on actors, directors, and producers. Visit the SAG website for more information.

Screen Actors Guild (SAG)
5757 Wilshire Boulevard
Los Angeles, CA 90036-3600
Tel: 323-954-1600
http://www.sag.com

For information about opportunities in not-for-profit theaters, contact

Theatre Communications Group
520 Eighth Avenue
New York, NY 10018-4156
Tel: 212-609-5900
Email: tcg@tcg.org
http://www.tcg.org

This site has information for beginners on acting and the acting business.

Acting Workshop On-Line
http://www.redbirdstudio.com/AWOL/acting2.html

Animators

QUICK FACTS

School Subjects
Art
Computer science

Personal Skills
Artistic
Communication/ideas

Work Environment
Primarily indoors
Primarily one location

Minimum Education Level
High school diploma

Salary Range
$29,030 to $74,980 to
$94,260+

Certification or Licensing
None available

Outlook
About as fast as the average

DOT
141

GOE
01.04.02

NOC
5241

O*NET-SOC
27-1014.00

OVERVIEW

Animators are artists who design the cartoons that appear in movies, television shows, and commercials.

HISTORY

Frenchmen Emile Reynaud created what is considered the first animated cartoon in 1892. He created the cartoon by drawing and hand-painting images on film paper and using a praxinoscope, an optical instrument he invented to create the illusion of movement, or animation. *Fantasmagorie*, considered the first fully animated film, was made by French director Emile Courtet (aka Emile Cohl) in 1908.

As Hollywood grew in the early 1900s, so did companies that created cartoons, although these animated films were silent (just like all movies of the time). Bray Studios in New York City was one of the best-known cartoon studios of the time. It operated from circa 1915 to the late 1920s. Some of its cartoons include *Out of the Inkwell* (1916), *Electric Bell* (1918), and *If You Could Shrink* (1920).

Walt Disney also got his start in the business around this time. In 1923, he sold his first cartoon, *Alice's Wonderland*, to a distributor and soon after founded Disney Brothers Cartoon Studio (later renamed Walt Disney Studio) with his brother, Roy. By the late 1920s "talkies" had replaced silent films and Walt Disney had created the cartoon character, Mickey Mouse, which still entertains young and old to this day.

The 1930s and 1940s are considered the golden age of animation. The Walt Disney Studio dominated the industry during these decades. During this time, it created the first animated feature film, *Snow*

White and the Seven Dwarfs, which debuted in 1937. The animated film was so groundbreaking that the Academy of Motion Pictures and Sciences gave it a special award in 1938, stating: "to Walt Disney for *Snow White and the Seven Dwarfs*, recognized as a significant screen innovation which has charmed millions and pioneered a great new entertainment field for the motion picture cartoon." Walt Disney Studio went on to create many other animated feature-length classics, including *Pinocchio, Fantasia,* and *Dumbo.*

The popularity of television in the 1950s caused a decline in interest in theatrical cartoons and feature films that lasted into the 1980s. Many consider the release of *Who Framed Roger Rabbit?* by Walt Disney Studio in 1988 as the beginning of a renaissance in animation that continues to this day. Major animation trends over the last two decades include the popularity of adult-oriented animation, such as *The Simpsons* and *South Park*; the emergence of *anime* [Japanese-based (although the phenomena has spread throughout Asia) high-quality animation in a variety of genres that is geared not just toward children, but adults, too]; the creation of cable networks, such as Nickelodeon and the Cartoon Network, that offer animation as much or all of their programming; and the rise of computer-generated animation, which allows animators infinite creative options and the ability to complete animated features in far less time than by using traditional methods.

THE JOB

Animators, often called *motion cartoonists*, design the cartoons that appear in films and television shows. They also create the digital effects for many films and commercials. Computer animators created more than 2,000 of the effects in *Star Wars: Episode I—The Phantom Menace*. Making a big budget animated film, such as *A Bug's Life* or *Shrek*, requires a team of many creative people. Each animator on the team works on one small part of the film. On a small production, animators may be involved in many different aspects of the project's development.

An animated film begins with a script. *Screenwriters* plan the story line, or plot, and write it with dialogue and narration. *Designers* read the script and decide how the film should look—should it be realistic, futuristic, or humorous? They then draw some of the characters and backgrounds. These designs are then passed on to a *storyboard artist* who illustrates the whole film in a series of frames, similar to a very long comic strip. Based on this storyboard, an artist can then create a detailed layout.

The most common form of animation is *cell animation.* Animators examine the script, the storyboard, and the layout and begin to prepare the finished artwork frame by frame, or cell by cell, on a combination of paper and transparent plastic sheets. Some animators create the "key" drawings—these are the drawings that capture the characters' main expressions and gestures at important parts in the plot. Other animators create the "in between" drawings—the drawings that fill in the spaces between one key drawing and the next. The thousands of final black and white cells are then scanned into a computer. With computer programs, animators add color, special effects, and other details.

In *stop-motion animation,* an object such as a clay creature or doll is photographed, moved slightly, and photographed again. The process is repeated hundreds of thousands of times. Movies such as *Chicken Run* were animated this way. In computer or digital animation, the animator creates all the images directly on the computer screen. Computer programs can create effects like shadows, reflections, distortions, and dissolves.

Animators are relying increasingly on computers in various areas of production. Computers are used to color animation art, whereas formerly, every frame was painted by hand. Computers also help animators create special effects or even entire films. (One program, Macromedia's Flash, has given rise to an entire Internet cartoon subculture.)

Other people who work in animation are *prop designers*, who create objects used in animated films, and *layout artists*, who visualize and create the world that cartoon characters inhabit.

REQUIREMENTS

High School
If you are interested in becoming an animator, you should, of course, take art as well as computer classes in high school. Math classes, such as algebra and geometry, will also be helpful. If your school offers graphic design classes, be sure to take those.

Postsecondary Training
You do not need to go to college to become an animator, but there are a number of animation programs offered at universities and art institutes across the country. You may choose to pursue a bachelor's, a master's of fine art, or a Ph.D. in computer animation, digital art, graphic design, or art. Some of today's top computer animators are self-taught or have learned their skills on the job.

An animator edits an animated feature in a studio in Tokyo, Japan.
(Tom Wagner, Corbis SABA)

Other Requirements

Animators must be creative. In addition to having artistic talent, they must generate ideas, although it is not unusual for animators to collaborate with writers for ideas. They must have a good sense of humor (or a good dramatic sense) and an observant eye to detect people's distinguishing characteristics and society's interesting attributes or incongruities.

Animators need to be flexible. Because their art is commercial, they must be willing to accommodate their employers' desires if they are to build a broad clientele and earn a decent living. They must be able to take suggestions and rejections gracefully.

EXPLORING

Ask your high school art or computer teacher to arrange a presentation by an animator, or if you live near an animation studio, try to arrange a tour of a production facility. Sketch as much as you possibly can. Carry a sketchpad around in order to quickly capture images and gestures that seem interesting to you. There are many computer animation software programs available that teach basic principles and techniques. Experiment with these programs to create basic animation. Some video cameras have stop-motion buttons that allow you to take a series of still shots. You can use this feature to experiment with claymation and other stop-motion techniques.

Useful Websites for Animators

Animated News
http://www.animated-news.com

Animation Artist
http://www.animationartist.com

Animation Insider
http://www.animationinsider.net

Animation Magazine
http://www.animationmagazine.net

Animation World Network
http://www.awn.com

DreamWorks Animation
http://www.dreamworksanimation.com

Pixar
http://www.pixar.com

StopMotionAnimation.com
http://www.stopmotionanimation.com

EMPLOYERS

Employers of animators include producers, movie studios, and television networks. In addition, a number of these artists are self-employed, working on a freelance basis. Some do animation on the Web as a part-time business or a hobby. Others work for computer game companies.

STARTING OUT

A few places, such as the Walt Disney Studio, offer apprenticeships. To enter these programs, applicants must have attended an accredited art school for two or three years.

One new way up-and-coming animators have made themselves known to the animating community is by attracting an audience on the World Wide Web. A portfolio of well-executed Web 'toons can help an animator build his reputation and get jobs. Some animators, such as the

Brothers Chaps (creators of http://www.homestarrunner.com), have even been able to turn their creations into a profitable business.

ADVANCEMENT

Animators' success, like that of other artists, depends on how much the public likes their work. Very successful animators work for well-known film companies and other employers at the best wages; some become well known to the public.

EARNINGS

According to the U.S. Department of Labor, multimedia artists and animators who were employed in the motion picture and video industries earned an annual mean salary of $74,980 in 2004. Salaries for all multimedia artists and animators ranged from less than $29,030 to more than $94,260. Cel painters, as listed in a salary survey conducted by *Animation World,* start at about $750 a week; animation checkers, $930 a week; story sketchers, $1,500 weekly.

Self-employed artists do not receive fringe benefits such as paid vacations, sick leave, health insurance, or pension benefits. Those who are salaried employees of companies and the like do typically receive these fringe benefits.

WORK ENVIRONMENT

Most animators work in big cities where movie and television studios are located. They generally work in comfortable environments with good light. Staff animators work a regular 40-hour workweek but may occasionally be expected to work evenings and weekends to meet deadlines. Freelance animators have erratic schedules, and the number of hours they work may depend on how much money they want to earn or how much work they can find. They often work evenings and weekends but are not required to be at work during regular office hours.

Animators can be frustrated by employers who curtail their creativity, asking them to follow instructions that are contrary to what they would most like to do. Many freelance animators spend a lot of time working alone at home, but animators have more opportunities to interact with other people than do most working artists.

OUTLOOK

Employment for artists and related workers is expected to grow at a rate about as fast as the average through 2012, according to the U.S.

Department of Labor. The growing trend of sophisticated special effects in motion pictures should create opportunities at industry effects houses such as Sony Pictures Imageworks, DreamQuest Software, Industrial Light & Magic, and DreamWorks SKG. Furthermore, growing processor and Internet connection speeds are creating a Web animation renaissance. Because so many creative and talented people are drawn to this field, however, competition for jobs will be strong.

Animated features are not just for children anymore. Much of the animation today is geared for an adult audience. Interactive computer games, animated films, network and cable television, and the Internet are among the many employment sources for talented animators. More than half of all visual artists are self-employed, but freelance work can be hard to come by, and many freelancers earn little until they acquire experience and establish a good reputation. Competition for work will be keen; those with an undergraduate or advanced degree in art or film will be in demand. Experience in action drawing and computers is a must.

FOR MORE INFORMATION

For membership and scholarship information, contact
International Animated Film Society
2114 Burbank Boulevard
Burbank, CA 91506
Tel: 818-842-8330
Email: asifaalert-subscribe@yahoogroups.com
http://www.asifa-hollywood.org

For an art school directory, a scholarship guide, and general information, contact
National Art Education Association
1916 Association Drive
Reston, VA 20191-1590
Tel: 703-860-8000
Email: naea@dgs.dgsys.com
http://www.naea-reston.org

For an overview of animation and useful exercises, visit the following website:
Animating: Creating Movement Frame by Frame
http://www.oscars.org/teachersguide/animation/download.html

Art Directors

OVERVIEW

In films, videos, and television commercials, *art directors* set the general look of the visual elements and approve the props, costumes, and models. In addition, they are involved in casting, editing, and selecting the music. In film and video, the art director is usually an experienced animator or computer/graphic arts designer who supervises animators or other artistic staff. They supervise both in-house and off-site staff, handle executive issues, and oversee the entire artistic production process. There are more than 149,000 artists and art directors working in the United States.

HISTORY

Artists have always been an important part of the creative process throughout history. Medieval monks illuminated their manuscripts, painting with egg-white tempera on vellum. Each copy of each book had to be printed and illustrated individually.

Printed illustrations first appeared in books in 1461. Through the years, prints were made through woodblock, copperplate, lithography, and other means of duplicating images. Although making many copies of the same illustration was now possible, publishers still depended on individual artists to create the original works. Text editors usually decided what was to be illustrated and how, while artists commonly supervised the production of the artwork.

The first art directors were probably staff illustrators for book publishers. As the publishing industry grew more complex and incorporated new technologies such as photography and film, art direction evolved into a more supervisory position and became a full-time job.

Publishers and advertisers began to need specialists who could acquire and use illustrations and photos.

With the creation of animation, art directors became more indispensable than ever. Animated short films, such as the early Mickey Mouse cartoons, were usually supervised by art directors. Walt Disney himself was the art director on many of his early pictures. And as full-length films have moved into animation, the sheer number of illustrations requires more than one art director to oversee the project.

Today's art directors supervise almost every type of visual project produced. Through a variety of methods and media, from television and film to magazines, comic books, and the Internet, art directors communicate ideas by selecting and supervising every element that goes into the finished product.

THE JOB

Art directors are responsible for all visual aspects of on-screen or printed projects. The art director oversees the process of developing visual solutions to a variety of communication problems. He or she creates film and video productions, television commercials, and websites; helps to establish corporate identities; advertises products and services; and enhances books, magazines, newsletters, and other publications. Some art directors with experience or knowledge in specific fields specialize in such areas as packaging, exhibitions and displays, or the Internet. But all directors, even those with specialized backgrounds, must be skilled in and knowledgeable about design, illustration, photography, computers, research, and writing in order to supervise the work of graphic artists, photographers, copywriters, text editors, and other employees.

In film and video and broadcast advertising, the art director has a wide variety of responsibilities and often interacts with an enormous number of creative professionals. Working with directors, producers, and other professionals, art directors interpret scripts and create or select settings in order to visually convey the story or the message. The art director oversees and channels the talents of set decorators and designers, model makers, location managers, propmasters, construction coordinators, and special effects people. In addition, art directors work with writers, unit production managers, cinematographers, costume designers, and post-production staff, including editors and employees responsible for scoring and titles. The art director is ultimately responsible for all visual aspects of the finished product.

The process of producing the look of a motion picture begins in much the same way that a printed advertising piece is created. The art director may start with the director or producer's concept or create one in-house in collaboration with staff members. Once a concept has been created, the art director sketches a rough storyboard based on the director or producer's ideas, and the plan is presented for review to those involved. The next step is to develop a finished storyboard, with larger and more detailed frames (the individual scenes) in color. This storyboard is presented to the client for review and used as a guide for the film director as well.

Technology is playing an increasingly important role in the art director's job. Most art directors, for example, use a variety of computer software programs, including Adobe PageMaker, FrameMaker, Illustrator, and Photoshop; Macromedia Dreamweaver; QuarkXPress; and CorelDRAW. Many others create and oversee websites for clients and work with other interactive media and materials, including CD-ROM, touch-screens, multidimensional visuals, and new animation programs.

Art directors usually work on more than one project at a time and must be able to keep numerous, unrelated details straight. They often work under pressure of a deadline and yet must remain calm and pleasant when dealing with clients and staff. Because they are supervisors, art directors are often called upon to resolve problems, not only with projects but with employees as well.

Art directors are not entry-level workers. They usually have years of experience working at lower-level jobs in the field before gaining the knowledge needed to supervise projects. Depending on whether they work primarily in film or publishing, art directors have to know how film is processed or digitally mastered or how printing presses operate. They should also be familiar with a variety of production techniques in order to understand the wide range of ways that images can be manipulated to meet the needs of a project.

REQUIREMENTS

High School

A college degree is usually a requirement for art directors; however, in some instances, it is not absolutely necessary. A variety of high school courses will give you both a taste of college-level offerings and an idea of the skills necessary for art directors on the job. These courses include art, drawing, art history, graphic design, illustration, photography, advertising, and desktop publishing.

Other useful courses that you should take in high school include business, computing, drama, English, technical drawing, cultural studies, psychology, and social science.

Postsecondary Training

Courses in photography, filmmaking, set direction, advertising, marketing, layout, desktop publishing, and fashion are also important for those interested in becoming art directors. Specialized courses, sometimes offered only at professional film or art schools, may be particularly helpful for students who want to go into art direction. These include animation, storyboard, typography, website design, and portfolio development.

Because of the rapidly increasing use of computers in design work, it is essential to have a thorough understanding of how computer art and layout programs work. In smaller companies, the art director may be responsible for operating this equipment; in larger companies, a staff person, under the direction of the art director, may use these programs. In either case, the director must know what can be done with the available equipment.

In addition to course work at the college level, many universities and professional art schools offer graduates or students in their final year a variety of workshop projects, desktop publishing training opportunities, and internships. These programs provide students with opportunities to develop their personal design styles as well as their portfolios.

Other Requirements

The work of an art director requires creativity, imagination, curiosity, and a sense of adventure. Art directors must be able to work with all sorts of specialized equipment and computer software, such as graphic design programs, as well as make presentations on the ideas behind their work.

The ability to work well with different people and organizations is a must for art directors. They must always be up-to-date on new techniques, trends, and attitudes. And because deadlines are a constant part of the work, an ability to handle stress and pressure well is key.

Other requirements for art directors include time management skills and an interest in media and people's motivations and lifestyles.

EXPLORING

High school students can get an idea of what an art director does by working on the staff of the school newspaper, magazine, or yearbook, and developing their own websites or zines. It may also be possible to secure a part-time job assisting the advertising director of the local newspaper or to work at an advertising agency. Developing your own artistic talent is important, and this can be accomplished through self-training (reading books and practicing); through courses in painting, drawing, or other creative arts; or by working with a group of friends to create a movie. At the very least, you should develop your "creative eye," that is, your ability to develop ideas visually. One way to do this is by familiarizing yourself with great works, such as paintings or highly creative motion pictures, videos, or commercials.

EMPLOYERS

A variety of organizations in virtually all industries employ art directors. Art directors who oversee and produce on-screen products often work for film production houses, Web designers, multimedia developers, computer game developers, or television stations. Others might work at advertising agencies, publishing houses, museums, packaging firms, photography studios, marketing and public relations firms, desktop publishing outfits, digital prepress houses, or printing companies.

STARTING OUT

Since an art director's job requires a great deal of experience, it is usually not considered an entry-level position. Typically, a person on a career track toward art director is hired as an assistant to an established director. Recent graduates wishing to enter the field should have a portfolio containing samples of their work to demonstrate their understanding of both the business and the media in which they want to work.

Serving as an intern is a good way to get experience and develop skills. Graduates should also consider taking an entry-level job at a film studio or in a publisher's art department to gain initial experience. Either way, aspiring art directors must be willing to acquire their credentials by working on various projects. This may mean working in a variety of areas, such as advertising, marketing, editing, and design.

ADVANCEMENT

While some may be content upon reaching the position of art director to remain there, many art directors take on even more responsibility within their organizations, become film or television directors, start their own advertising agencies, create their own websites, develop original multimedia programs, or launch their own magazines.

Many people who get to the position of art director do not advance beyond the title but move on to work on more prestigious films or at better known firms. Competition for top positions continues to be keen because of the sheer number of talented people interested. At smaller publications or local companies, the competition may be less intense, since candidates are competing primarily against others in the local market.

EARNINGS

According to the U.S. Department of Labor, a beginning art director or an art director working at a small firm can expect to make $35,500 or less per year in 2004, with experienced art directors working at larger companies earning more than $123,320. Mean annual earnings for art directors employed in the motion picture and video industries were $95,380 in 2004.

Most companies employing art directors offer insurance benefits, a retirement plan, and other incentives and bonuses. Freelance art directors employed in the motion picture and television industries are usually responsible for providing their own health insurance and other benefits.

WORK ENVIRONMENT

Art directors usually work in studios or office buildings. While their work areas are ordinarily comfortable, well lit, and ventilated, they often handle glue, paint, ink, and other materials that pose safety hazards, and they should, therefore, exercise caution.

Art directors at art and design studios and publishing firms usually work a standard 40-hour week. Many, however, work overtime during busy periods in order to meet deadlines. Similarly, directors at film and video operations and at television studios work as many hours as required—usually many more than 40 per week—in order to finish projects according to predetermined schedules.

While art directors work independently while reviewing artwork and reading copy, much of their time is spent collaborating with and supervising a team of employees, often consisting of copywriters, editors, photographers, graphic artists, and account executives.

OUTLOOK

The extent to which art director positions are in demand, like many other positions, depends on the economy in general; when times are tough, people and businesses spend less, and cutbacks are made. When the economy is healthy, employment prospects for art directors will be favorable. The U.S. Department of Labor predicts that employment for art directors will grow about as fast as the average for all other occupations. Creators of films and videos need images in order to produce their programs, and people working with new media are increasingly looking for artists and directors to promote new and existing products and services, enhance their websites, develop new multimedia programs, and create multidimensional visuals. People who can quickly and creatively generate new concepts and ideas will be in high demand.

However, it is important to note that the supply of aspiring artists is expected to exceed the number of job openings. As a result, those wishing to enter the field will encounter keen competition for salaried, staff positions as well as for freelance work. And although the Internet is expected to provide many opportunities for artists and art directors, some firms are hiring employees without formal art or design training to operate computer-aided design systems and oversee work.

FOR MORE INFORMATION

For more information on design professionals, contact
American Institute of Graphic Arts
164 Fifth Avenue
New York, NY 10010
Tel: 212-807-1990
http://www.aiga.org

The Art Directors Club is an international, nonprofit organization of directors in advertising, graphic design, interactive media, broadcast design, typography, packaging, environmental design, photography, illustration, and related disciplines. For information, contact
Art Directors Club
106 West 29th Street
New York, NY 10001
Tel: 212-643-1440
Email: info@adcglobal.org
http://www.adcglobal.org

For information on the graphic arts, contact
Graphic Artists Guild
90 John Street, Suite 403
New York, NY 10038-3202
Tel: 212-791-3400
http://www.gag.org

━━━━━━ INTERVIEW ━━━━━━

Karen Fletcher Trujillo has had a varied career in the film industry. She has worked as a set designer for such films as Home Alone, Groundhog Day, *and* Dennis the Menace; *an art director on films such as* My Best Friend's Wedding *and* Light It Up; *and currently teaches production design at Columbia College Chicago. Karen was kind enough to discuss her interesting career with the editors of* Careers in Focus: Film.

Q. What is the difference between a set designer and an art director?

A. Production designers are responsible for the entire look of the film, including sets, locations, set decorating, costumes, props, hair, and makeup. Art directors are generally responsible for the completion of the sets, communicating the production designer's wishes to the construction coordinator, completion of drawings, surveying of locations, coordination of schedules in advance of shooting dates, and building, prep, and strike of sets.

Q. How long have you been an educator? What classes do you typically teach?

A. I have been teaching at Columbia for five years, two semesters a year. I teach the only production design course at Columbia, Production Design: Features.

Q. Tell us about your career before you began to teach.

A. I have a degree in architecture from Syracuse University, but have always been interested in theater. I did the exercises from *What Color Is Your Parachute?*, by Richard Bolles, and came up with the title of art director from the *Dictionary of Occupational Titles*. I learned how to network from the book and after my fourth cold call I was hired as a set designer on *Home Alone*. I worked for 10 years as a set designer on various features shooting here in Chicago. The last two films I did as an art director were *My Best Friend's Wedding* and *Light It Up*—both with Academy Award–

winning production designers. I have production designed a couple of films which never got to completion.

Q. What are the most important qualities of a successful film in terms of production design?

A. I would say the most important quality is supporting the idea of the story. Some films are just not production design-oriented, but the designer must think beyond that to the background story and in conjunction with the ideas of the director and cinematographer. Also, doing what you can within budget. I teach my students not to compromise their ideas because of budget; just reach for the sky, then bring it back within reason and you'll end up with something better than you thought.

Q. What are the most important personal qualities for successful production designers?

A. Some of the most important qualities for a designer are organization, flexibility, and a sense of style; the ability to translate words into pictures or models that communicate (which can be learned); and the ability to prioritize and back up your decisions.

Q. What advice would you offer graduates as they prepare to break into the field?

A. I would advise them to take courses in theater, architecture, animation, editing, and fine art; get on to professionally run films in the art department to get as much experience as possible; and work on student films to make contacts for the future, but don't get caught just moving furniture around.

Audio Recording Engineers

OVERVIEW

Audio recording engineers oversee the technical end of recording. They operate the controls of the recording equipment—often under the direction of a music producer—during the production of film, television, and radio productions; music recordings; and other mediums that require sound recording. Recording engineers monitor and operate electronic and computer consoles to make necessary adjustments, and solve technical problems as they occur during a recording session. They assure that the equipment is in optimal working order and obtain any additional equipment necessary for the recording. Approximately 90,000 broadcast and sound engineering technicians are employed in the United States.

HISTORY

The job of the contemporary audio recording engineer as we know it began in the late 1940s with the development of magnetic tape as a recording medium. Tape provided a new and flexible method for recording engineers to influence the outcome of the recording session. Before tape, records were cut on warm wax blanks that allowed only minimal manipulation of sound quality. Generally, whatever the musicians produced in the recording studio is what came out on the record, and the degree of quality rested almost entirely in the hands of the studio engineer.

The innovation of tape and the introduction of long-playing (LP) records brought significant improvements to the recording industry.

Since tape allowed recording on multiple tracks, recording engineers were now needed to edit and enhance tape quality and "mix" each track individually to produce a balanced sound on all tracks. Tape allowed recording engineers to perform patchwork corrections to a recording by replacing sections where musician errors or poor sound quality occurred.

By the 1950s recording engineers played a vital role in the record industry. The emergence of rock and roll brought an explosion of recordings in the industry, and each recording required a technically proficient, creative, and skilled audio recording engineer. Although engineers often had to produce sounds at the direction of the music producer, many worked at their own discretion and produced truly unique sounds. Engineers also found employment for film productions in Hollywood and for radio station productions throughout the United States.

The development of music-related software for the computer has altered many aspects of music recording, particularly in the editing process. Many time-consuming tasks previously performed manually can now be done in half the time and less with new specially programmed software. More than ever before, today's audio recording engineer must be highly educated and up-to-date with the rapidly changing technology that ultimately affects the way he or she performs the job.

THE JOB

Audio recording engineers operate and maintain the equipment used in a sound recording studio. They record: music, live and in studios; speech, such as dramatic readings of novels or radio advertisements; and sound effects and dialogue used in film and television. They work in control rooms at master console boards often containing hundreds of dials, switches, meters, and lights, which the engineer reads and adjusts to achieve desired results during a recording. Today, the recording studio is often considered an extra instrument, and thus, the audio recording engineer becomes an extra musician in his or her ability to dramatically alter the final sound of the recording.

As recording engineers prepare to record a session, they ask the film or television director, musicians, producer, or whoever has hired them what style of music will be played and what type of sound and emotion they want reflected in the final recording. Audio recording engineers must find out what types of instruments and orchestration will be recorded to determine how to manage the recording session and what additional equipment will be needed. For example, each instrument or vocalist may require a special microphone. The recording of dialogue will take considerably less preparation.

Before the recording session, audio recording engineers test all microphones, cords, recording equipment, and amplifiers to ensure everything is operating correctly. They load tape players and set recording levels. Microphones must be positioned in precise locations near the instrument or amplifier. They experiment with several different positions of the microphone and listen in the control room for the best sound. Depending on the size of the studio and the number of musicians or vocalists, audio recording engineers position musicians in various arrangements to obtain the best sound for the production. For smaller projects, such as three- to eight-piece bands, each instrument may be sectioned off in soundproof rooms to ensure the sounds of one instrument do not "bleed" into the recording of another instrument. For more complex recording of larger orchestration, specialized microphones must be placed in exact locations to record one or several instruments.

Once audio recording engineers have the musicians in place and the microphones set, they instruct musicians to play a sample of their music. At the main console, they read the gauges and set recording levels for each instrument. Recording engineers must listen for sound imperfections, such as hissing, popping, "mike bleeding," and any other extraneous noises, and pinpoint their source. They turn console dials to adjust recording level, volume, tone, and effects. Depending on the problem, they may have to reposition either the microphone or the musician.

With the right sound and recording level of each microphone set, audio recording engineers prepare the recording equipment (either tape or digital). During the recording of a song or voice-over, they monitor the recording level of each microphone to ensure none of the tracks are too high, which results in distortion, or too low, which results in weak sound quality. Recording engineers usually record more than one "take" of a song. Before the mixing process, they listen to each take carefully and determine which one has the best sound. They often splice the best part of one take with the best part of another take.

In some recording sessions, two engineers work in the control room. One usually works with the recording equipment, and the other takes instruction from the producer. The engineers coordinate the ideas of the producer to create the desired sound. During each session, the volume, speed, intensity, and tone quality must be carefully monitored. Producers may delegate more responsibility to the recording engineer. Engineers often tell the musicians when to start and stop playing or when to redo a certain section. They may ask musicians or other studio technicians to move microphones or other equipment in the studio to improve sound quality.

After the recording is made, the individual tracks must be "mixed" to a master tape. When mixing, the audio recording engineers balance each instrument in relation to the others. Together with the film director, producer, musicians, or others who have hired them, recording engineers listen to the song or piece several times with the instruments at different levels and decide on the best sound and consistency. At this stage, they also set equalization and manipulate sound, tone, intensity, effects, and speed of the recording.

Audio recording engineers frequently perform maintenance and repair on their equipment. They must identify and solve common technical problems in the studio. They may have to rewire or move equipment when updating the studio with new equipment. They may write proposals for equipment purchases and studio design changes. Engineers are often assisted in many of the basic sound recording tasks by apprentices, who are also known as *studio technicians*.

Recording engineers at smaller studios may set studio times for musicians. They must keep a thorough account of the band or performer scheduled to play, the musical style of the band or performer, the specific equipment that will be needed, and any other special arrangements needed to make the session run smoothly. They make sure the studio is stocked with the right working accessory equipment, including cords, cables, microphones, amplifiers, tapes, tuners, and effect pedals.

REQUIREMENTS

High School
You should take music courses to learn an instrument, study voice, or learn composition. High school orchestras and bands are an excellent source for both practicing and studying music performance. You should also take classes in computer science, mathematics, business, and, if offered, electronics. A drama or broadcast journalism class may allow you access to a sound booth, and the opportunity to assist with audio engineering for live theatrical productions and radio programs.

Postsecondary Training
More than ever before, postsecondary training is an essential step for becoming a successful recording engineer. This is when you will make your first contacts and be introduced to many of the highly technical

(and continually changing) aspects of the field. To learn about educational opportunities in the United States and abroad, visit the websites of the Audio Engineering Society (http://www.aes.org) or *Mix* Magazine Online (http://www.mixonline.com).

Seminars and workshops offer the most basic level of education. This may be the best way to obtain an early, hands-on understanding of audio recording and prepare for entry-level apprentice positions. These programs are intended to introduce students to the equipment and technical aspects of the field, such as microphones, sound reinforcement, audio processing devices, tape and DAT machines, digital processing, and sound editing. Students will also become familiar with the newest technologies in the audio field, such as MIDI (musical instrument digital interface), synthesis, sampling, and current music software. A seminar can last from a couple of hours to several weeks. Many workshops are geared toward in-depth study of a certain aspect of recording such as mixing, editing, or music production.

Students looking for a more comprehensive course of study in specific areas of the recording industry can enroll in technical school or community college programs. Depending on the curriculum, these programs can take from several weeks to up to a year to complete. The most complete level of postsecondary education is a two- or four-year degree from a university. At many universities, students have access to state-of-the-art equipment and a teaching staff of knowledgeable professionals in the industry. Universities incorporate music, music technology, and music business in a comprehensive curriculum that prepare graduates to be highly competitive in the industry. Students can enroll in other nonaudio courses, such as business, communications, marketing, and computers.

Certification or Licensing

In the broadcast industry, engineers can be certified by the Society of Broadcast Engineers (http://www.sbe.org). Certification is recommended because this step shows your dedication to the field and your level of competence. After completing technical training and meeting strict qualifications, you can also join the Society as a member or associate member. Membership gives you access to educational seminars, conferences, and a weekly job line.

Other Requirements

Being a recording engineer requires both technical skills and communication skills. You must be patient, capable of working well with a variety of people, and possess the confidence to function in a leadership position. Excellent troubleshooting skills are essential for an audio recording engineer.

EXPLORING

One way to learn more about this field is to read publications that focus on audio recording. *Mix* Magazine Online (http://www.mixonline.com) offers articles about education, technology, and production. Other publications that provide useful information on the industry and audio recording techniques include *Remix* (http://www.remixmag.com), *Pro Sound News* (http://www.prosoundnews.com), and *Broadcast Engineering* (http://www.broadcastengineering.com).

Any experience you can get working in or around music will provide excellent background for this field. You could take up an instrument in the school band or orchestra, or perform with your own band. You might also have the opportunity to work behind the scenes with a music group, serving as a business manager, helping set up sound systems, or working as a technician in a school sound recording studio or radio station.

If you are interested in entering the film industry, write or call film companies or recording studios that work with motion picture audio recording to get more information; local studios can usually be found in the classified telephone directory, and others can be located in the music trade magazines. The National Academy of Recording Arts and Sciences (the organization responsible for the Grammy Awards) is one source for information on the industry. Numerous books and music trade magazines that cover music production are available at bookstores or libraries.

EMPLOYERS

Approximately 90,000 broadcast and sound engineering technicians are employed in the United States. Sixteen percent of these workers are employed in the motion picture and sound recording industries. Though most major recording studios are located in metropolitan areas such as New York and Los Angeles, many cities across the country have vibrant music scenes. Talented, skilled engineers will always be in demand, no matter the size of the recording studio. They may be employed by a studio, or they may be self-employed, either contracting with studios or operating their own recording business. Engineers also work for broadcast companies, engineering sound for radio and TV programs. Some recording engineers work for video production companies and corporate media libraries, helping to create in-house company presentations and films. Other work as freelancers in the film industry.

STARTING OUT

After high school, seek experience as an intern or apprentice or begin postsecondary training in audio at a university, college, or trade school. Because most professional recording studios and broadcasters prefer to offer apprenticeship positions to students who have some previous experience in audio, those who have completed some trade school courses may have better chances at landing jobs. Most university and college programs offer semester internship programs at professional recording studios as a way of earning credit. Professional trade associations also support internships for their members by either matching students with employers or funding internship expenses. Universities and trade schools also have job placement services for their graduates.

Internships and apprenticeships play an important role in helping students establish personal connections. Students are often hired by the studios or stations with which they've interned or their employer can make recommendations for other job openings at a different studio. Employers will often post entry-level openings at universities or trade schools, but very seldom will they advertise in a newspaper.

Most audio engineers begin their career in small studios as assistants, called studio technicians, and have varied responsibilities, which may entail anything from running out to pick up dinner for the musicians during a recording session, to helping the recording engineer in the mixing process. Positions in radio will also provide a good stepping-stone to a career in audio recording. Entry-level positions may be easier to come by at studios that specialize in educational recording and radio advertisements than at music recording studios.

ADVANCEMENT

Career advancement will depend upon an engineer's interests as well as on hard work and perseverance. They may advance to the higher paying, glamorous (yet high-pressure) position of music producer, either as an independent producer or working for a record label. Recording engineers may also advance to positions in the radio or television industries, which usually offer better pay than studio work. If engineers wish to stay in the field of audio recording, they can advance to managerial positions or choose to open their own recording studio. Recording engineers who are already employed in the film industry may advance by working with more prestigious directors or on larger-budget movies.

The recording industry is continually changing in response to frequent technological breakthroughs. Recording engineers who adapt easily to such advances as digital recording and new computer software will have a better chance for success. Some recording engineers may team up with producers who work independently of the studio. They may form their own company, allowing for greater flexibility and higher salaries.

EARNINGS

According to the U.S. Department of Labor, the mean income for sound engineering technicians employed in the motion picture and video industries was approximately $55,280 in 2004. Sound engineering technicians employed in all industries earned salaries that ranged from less than $19,180 to more than $80,450.

Benefits packages will vary from business to business. Audio recording engineers employed by a recording company or by a broadcast station receive health insurance and paid vacation. Other benefits may include dental and eye care, life and disability insurance, and a pension plan.

WORK ENVIRONMENT

Recording studios can be comfortable places to work. They are usually air-conditioned because of the sensitivity of the equipment. They may be loud or cramped, however, especially during recording sessions where many people are working in a small space. The work is not particularly demanding physically (except when recording engineers must move equipment), but there may be related stress depending on the personalities of the producer and the performers. Audio recording engineers must be able to follow directions from producers and must often give directions. Their work must be quick and precise, and the engineer must be able to work as part of a team. Depending on the type of recording business, some engineers may be required to record off-site where the recording is to take place. Engineers can usually come to work dressed however they wish.

Engineers must have patience when working with performers. For the engineer, there are often long periods of waiting while the musicians or performers work out problems and try to perfect parts of their songs. Engineers will frequently have to record the same song or spoken-word piece several times after mistakes have been made in the presentation. In addition, the mixing process itself can become tedious for many engineers—especially if they are not fond of the music. During the mix, engineers must listen to the same song over and over again to assure a proper balance of the musical tracks, and they often try various mixes.

Working hours depend on the job. Some studios are open at night or on the weekends to accommodate the schedules of musicians and performers. Other studios and recording companies only operate during normal business hours.

OUTLOOK

Employment in this field is expected to grow about as fast as the average through 2012, according to the U.S. Department of Labor. Growth should be especially strong for engineers who are employed in the motion picture industry—although competition will also be fierce as these jobs offer higher salaries and the opportunity to participate in what many view as the glamorous world of filmmaking. New computer technology (hardware and software) is rapidly changing the way many recording engineers perform their jobs, making the entire audio recording process easier. These technological advancements will negatively affect job prospects for entry-level studio technicians whose more mundane recording tasks will increasingly be performed by computers. However, technology will also have some beneficial impact. As American media expands through technology and markets such as digital cable open up, opportunities for audio recording engineers will likewise increase.

Competition for jobs will be steepest in high-paying urban areas. Audio recording engineers will find jobs more easily in small cities and towns.

FOR MORE INFORMATION

For information on graduate-level scholarships and audio recording schools and courses in the United States and abroad, contact
Audio Engineering Society
60 East 42nd Street, Room 2520
New York, NY 10165-2520
Tel: 212-661-8528
Email: HQ@aes.org
http://www.aes.org

For facts and statistics about the recording industry, contact
Recording Industry Association of America
1330 Connecticut Avenue, NW, Suite 300
Washington, DC 20036
Tel: 202-775-0101
http://www.riaa.com

For information on membership, contact
Society of Professional Audio Recording Services
9 Music Square South, Suite 222
Nashville, TN 37203
Tel: 800-771-7727
Email: spars@spars.com
http://www.spars.com

Camera Operators

QUICK FACTS

School Subjects
Art
Mathematics

Personal Skills
Communication/ideas
Mechanical/manipulative

Work Environment
Indoors and outdoors
Primarily multiple locations

Minimum Education Level
High school diploma

Salary Range
$15,730 to $50,590 to
$76,100+

Certification or Licensing
None available

Outlook
About as fast as the average

DOT
143

GOE
01.08.01

NOC
5222

O*NET-SOC
27-4031.00

OVERVIEW

Camera operators use motion picture cameras and equipment to photograph subjects or material for movies, television programs, or commercials. They usually use 35-millimeter or 16-millimeter cameras or camcorders and a variety of films, lenses, tripods, and filters in their work. Their instructions usually come from cinematographers or directors of photography (DPs). Approximately 28,000 camera operators work in the United States.

HISTORY

Motion pictures were made as early as 1877, using a series of still photographs to create the illusion of motion. But it was Thomas Edison who, in 1889, produced the first single-unit motion picture camera that set the standard for today.

The motion picture industry blossomed in the United States during the 20th century. With the growth of the television industry and the addition of commercial advertising to television, camera operators became indispensable members of the production crew. Motion picture directors and producers rely on camera operators to create the images on film that the directors and producers envision in their minds. As camera equipment becomes more complex and sophisticated, the camera operator will need to be more proficient at his or her craft.

THE JOB

Motion picture camera operators may work on feature films in Hollywood or on location elsewhere. Many work on educational films, documentaries, or television programs. The nature of the camera operator's work depends largely on the size of the production crew. If the film is a documentary or short news segment, the camera operator may be responsible for setting up the camera and lighting equipment as well as for supervising the actors during filming. Equipment that camera operators typically use include cranes, dollies, mounting heads, and different types of lenses and accessories. Often the camera operator is also responsible for maintenance and repair of all of this equipment.

With a larger crew, the camera operator is responsible only for the actual filming. The camera operator may even have a support team of assistants. The *first assistant camera operator* will typically focus on the cameras, making sure cameras are loaded and operating correctly and conferring with lighting specialists. In larger productions, there are also backup cameras and accessories for use if one should malfunction during filming. *Second assistant camera operators* help the first assistant set up scenes to be filmed and assist in the maintenance of the equipment.

Sometimes camera operators must use shoulder-held cameras. This often occurs during the filming of action scenes for television or motion pictures. *Special effects camera operators* photograph the optical effects segments for motion pictures and television. They create visual illusions that can add mood and tone to the motion picture. They usually add fades, dissolves, superimpositions, and other effects to their films at the request of the director of photography, also known as the director of cinematography or the cinematographer.

Brian Fass is a cinematographer/camera assistant in New York City. On a project, he works closely with the other professionals to help establish a visual style for the film. "During the project," he says, "I work on setting up the camera in various positions for coverage of scenes and then lighting each chosen angle." Fass has worked as a camera assistant for the Woody Allen films *Everyone Says I Love You* and *Deconstructing Harry,* as well as the Sidney Lumet film *Gloria.*

REQUIREMENTS

High School

Take classes that will prepare you for the technical aspect of the work—courses in photography, journalism, and media arts should give you some hands-on experience with a camera. Mathematics and science can help you in understanding cameras and filters. You should also take art and art history classes and other courses that will help you develop appreciation of visual styles.

Camera operators must be able to work closely with other members of a film crew during filming. Here, a camera operator discusses the setup of a shot with a cinematographer. *(Photo Disc)*

Postsecondary Training

A college degree is not necessary to get a position as a motion picture camera operator, but attending film school can help you expand your network of connections. A bachelor's degree in liberal arts or film studies provides a good background for work in the film industry, but practical experience and industry connections will provide the best opportunities for work. Upon completing an undergraduate program, you may wish to enroll in a master's program at a film school. Schools offering well-established programs include the School of Visual Arts in New York, New York University, and the University of Southern California. These schools have film professionals on their faculties and provide a very visible stage for student talent, being located in the two film business hot spots—New York and California. Film school offers overall formal training, providing an education in fundamental skills by working with student productions. Such education is rigorous, but in addition to teaching skills it provides you with peer groups and a network of contacts with students, faculty, and guest speakers that can be of help after graduation.

Other Requirements

You must be able to work closely with other members of a film crew and to carefully follow the instructions of the cinematographer and other camera operators. Since lighting is an integral part of filmmaking, you should have a thorough understanding of lighting equipment in order to work quickly and efficiently. In addition to the technical aspects of filmmaking, you should also understand the artistic nature of setting up shots. "I'm dyslexic and have always gravitated toward the visual mediums," Brian Fass says. "I feel that this impairment, along with my love of movies, made me turn toward cinematography."

EXPLORING

You should join a photography or camera club, or become involved with the media department of your school. You may have the opportunity then to videotape sports events, concerts, and school plays. You can also learn about photography by working in a camera shop. A part-time job in a camera shop will give you a basic understanding of photographic equipment. Some school districts have television stations where students can learn the basics of camera operation. This kind of hands-on experience is invaluable when it comes time to find work in the field. You can also learn about the film industry by reading such publications as *American Cinematographer* (http://www. theasc.com/magazine) and *Cinefex* (http://www.cinefex.com).

EMPLOYERS

There are approximately 28,000 television, video, and movie camera operators working in the United States. About 1 in 5 of these operators are self-employed. The majority of camera operators who are salaried employees work for the film and television industry at TV stations or film studios. Most jobs are found in large, urban areas.

STARTING OUT

Most entry-level jobs require little formal preparation in photography or camera operation. A college degree is not required by most film or television studios, but you may have to belong to the International Alliance of Theatrical Stage Employees (IATSE) Local 600, the national union for camera operators. An entry-level job as a camera assistant usually begins with assignments such as setting up or loading film into cameras and adjusting or checking lighting. With experience, the assistant may participate in decisions about what to photograph or how to film a particular scene.

Before you receive any paying jobs, you may have to work for awhile as a volunteer or intern on a film project. You can surf the

Read More about It

Carr, Jay, ed. *The A List: The National Society of Film Critics' 100 Essential Films.* Philadelphia: Da Capo Press, 2002.

Corey, Melinda, ed. *American Film Institute Desk Reference: The Complete Guide to Everything You Need to Know about the Movies.* New York: DK Publishing, 2002.

Karney, Robyn, Joel Finler, and Ronald Bergan, eds. *Cinema: Year by Year, 1894–2003.* New York: DK Publishing, 2003.

Osborne, Robert A. *75 Years of the Oscar: The Official History of the Academy Awards.* New York: Abbeville Press, 2003.

Stoller, Bryan Michael. *Filmmaking For Dummies.* New York: Wiley, 2003.

Taub, Eric. *Gaffers, Grips and Best Boys: From Producer-Director to Gaffer and Computer Special Effects Creator: A Behind-the-Scenes Look at Who Does What in the Making of a Motion Picture.* New York: St. Martin's Press, 1995.

Internet for postings of openings on film productions, or contact your state's film commission.

ADVANCEMENT

It usually takes two to four years for a motion picture camera operator to learn the techniques necessary for the job. Those who become proficient in their field, after several years of training, may be able to work on film projects as a cinematographer or director of photography. The DP supervises other camera operators and works more closely with the directors, producers, and actors in the creation of the film. Some camera operators study cinematography part-time while keeping their jobs as camera operators. They may later move to larger studios or command higher salaries.

"I work as an assistant for the money," Brian Fass says, "but hope to jump into work as a DP full time if the jobs come along. I also own my own Aaton XTR camera package, which makes me more marketable for DP jobs."

EARNINGS

Self-employed camera operators typically work on a project-by-project basis and may have periods of unemployment between jobs. Those working on movies may be paid per day, and their role in the creation of the movie may last anywhere from several weeks to several months. Camera operators who are salaried employees of, for example, a television network have steady, year-round employment. Because of these factors and others, such as area of the country in which the operator works and the size of the employer, salaries vary widely for these professionals. The U.S. Department of Labor reports the median annual earnings of all motion picture and video camera operators as $50,590 in 2004. The department also reports that the lowest paid 10 percent of all camera operators earned less than $15,730 per year, but at the top end of the pay scale, the highest earning 10 percent made more than $76,100 annually.

Salaried employees usually receive benefits such as health insurance, retirement plans, and vacation days. Those who are self-employed must pay for such extras themselves.

WORK ENVIRONMENT

Motion picture camera operators work indoors and outdoors. Most work for motion picture studios or in television broadcasting. During filming, a camera operator may spend several weeks or months on location in another city or country. Most often the camera operator lives and works in their home city and works during regular business hours. Hours can be erratic, however, if the film includes scenes that must be shot at night, or if a deadline must be met by after-hours filming.

Much of the work of a camera operator becomes routine after a few years of experience. Camera operators get used to loading and unloading film, carrying cameras and equipment from trucks or workshops into studios or sets, and filming segments over and over again. The glamour of working on motion pictures or television programs may be diminished by the physically demanding work. Also, the actors, directors, and producers are the individuals in the limelight. They often receive credit for the work the camera operators have done.

Many camera operators must be available to work on short notice. Since motion picture camera operators are generally hired to work on one film at a time, there may be long periods during which a camera operator is not working. Few can make a living as self-employed camera operators.

Motion picture camera operators working on documentary or news productions may work in dangerous places. Sometimes they must work in uncomfortable positions or make adjustments for imperfect lighting conditions. They usually operate their cameras while standing hours at a time. Deadline pressure is also a constant in the camera operator's work. Working for directors or producers who are on tight budgets or strict schedules may be very stressful.

OUTLOOK

Employment for camera operators is expected to increase about as fast as the average for all occupations through 2012, according to the U.S. Department of Labor. The use of visual images continues to grow in areas such as communication, education, entertainment, marketing, and research and development. More businesses will make use of video training films and public relations projects that use film. The entertainment industries are also expanding. However, competition for positions is very fierce. Camera operators work in what is considered a desirable and exciting field, and they must work hard and be aggressive to get good jobs, especially in Los Angeles and New York.

FOR MORE INFORMATION

For lists of tricks of the trade and favorite films of famous cinematographers, visit the ASC's website.

American Society of Cinematographers (ASC)
PO Box 2230
Hollywood, CA 90078
Tel: 800-448-0145
Email: info@theasc.com
http://www.theasc.com

For information on membership benefits, contact this branch of the International Alliance of Theatrical Stage Employees (IATSE).

International Cinematographers Guild (IATSE Local 600)
National Office/Western Region
7755 Sunset Boulevard, Suite 300
Hollywood, CA 90046
Tel: 323-876-0160
http://www.cameraguild.com

To learn about student chapters sponsored by the SMPTE, contact
   Society of Motion Picture and Television Engineers (SMPTE)
   3 Barker Avenue
   White Plains, NY 10601
   Tel: 914-761-1100
   Email: smpte@smpte.org
   http://www.smpte.org

*Visit this website organized by the ASC for a list of film schools and
to learn about the career of cinematographer—the next step on the
career ladder for camera operators.*
   Cinematographer.com
   http://www.cinematographer.com

Cinematographers and Directors of Photography

QUICK FACTS

School Subjects
Art
English

Personal Skills
Artistic
Technical/scientific

Work Environment
Indoors and outdoors
Primarily multiple locations

Minimum Education Level
Bachelor's degree

Salary Range
$15,730 to $50,590 to
$76,100+

Certification or Licensing
None available

Outlook
Faster than the average

DOT
143

GOE
01.08.01

NOC
5131

O*NET-SOC
27-4031.00

OVERVIEW

The *cinematographer,* also known as the *director of photography* or *DP*, is instrumental in establishing the mood of a film by putting the narrative aspects of a script into visual form. The cinematographer is responsible for every shot's framing, lighting, color level, and exposure—elements that set the artistic tone of the film.

HISTORY

Motion picture cameras were invented in the late 1800s. In 1903, Edwin Porter made *The Great Train Robbery,* the first motion picture that used modern filmmaking techniques to tell a story. Porter filmed the scenes out of sequence, and then edited and spliced them together to make the film, as is done today.

In the early years of film, the director handled the camera and made the artistic decisions that today are the job of the director of photography. The technical sophistication and artistic choices that are part of today's filming process had not yet emerged; instead, directors merely filmed narratives without moving the camera. Lighting was more for functional purposes of illumination than for artistic effect. Soon, however, directors began to experiment. They moved the camera to shoot from different angles and established a variety of editing techniques.

In the 1950s, the dominance of major studios in film production was curbed by an antitrust court decision, and more independent films were made. Changes in the U.S. tax code made independent producing more profitable. New genres and trends challenged the director and artistic staff of a production. Science fiction, adventure, mystery, and romance films grew in popularity. By the late 1960s, university film schools were established, training students in directing and cinematography as well as in other areas.

New developments in technologies and equipment have continued to influence both how films are made and how they look. The end of the 20th century and the beginning of the 21st saw the production of movies incorporating such elements as computer graphics, digital imaging, and digital color. Films such as *Titanic, Gladiator, Lord of the Rings,* and new "prequel" episodes of *Star Wars,* with their amount and complexity of their special effects, presented new visual challenges to filmmakers. Other films, such as *Toy Story, Shrek,* and *Finding Nemo,* are made entirely digitally. DPs lead the way in understanding and using new technologies to push the art of filmmaking into a new, digital era.

THE JOB

Cinematographers consider how the "look" of a film helps to tell its story. How can the look enhance the action, the emotions expressed, or the characters' personalities? Should the scene be filmed from across the room or up close to the actors? Should the lighting be stark or muted? How does the angle of the camera contribute to the scene? These are just some of the questions DPs must answer when composing a shot. Because DPs have both artistic and technical knowledge, they are integral members of the production team. They work in both film and television, helping directors to interpret a script and bring it to life.

At the beginning of a project, the DP reads the script and talks to the director about how to film each scene. Together they determine how to achieve the desired effects by deciding on camera angles and movement, lighting, framing, and which filters to use. By manipulating effects, DPs help determine the mood of a scene. For example, to raise the level of tension and discomfort in an argument, the DP can tell a camera operator to film at an unusual angle or move around the actors as they speak. The director may choose to film a scene in more than one way and then decide which best suits the project. With good collaboration between the director and the DP, decisions will be made quickly and successfully.

DPs are responsible for assembling the camera crew and telling crew members how to film each scene. They must be knowledgeable about all aspects of camera operation, lighting, filters, and types of film. There are multiple ways an effect can be approached, and DPs must be aware of them in order to make suggestions to the director and to capture the mood desired.

For small, low-budget films, some of the crew's roles may be combined. For example, the DP may operate a camera in addition to overseeing the crew. In a large production, the crew's roles will be more specialized. The *camera operator* either operates the camera physically or controls it remotely, using a control panel. The *first assistant camera operator* helps with focus, changes lenses and filters, sets the stop for film exposure, and makes sure the camera is working properly. Camera focus is extremely important and is not judged simply by how the shot looks to the eye. Instead, the first assistant carries a measuring tape and measures all the key positions of the actors and makes calculations to ensure correct focus. The *second assistant camera operator,* also called the *loader,* loads film magazines, keeps track of how much film stock is left, and keeps camera reports. Camera reports record which shots the director likes and wants to have printed. A *gaffer* leads the electrical crew, and the *grips* handle the dollies and cranes to move the cameras.

When shooting begins, cinematographers take a series of test shots of film locations to determine the lighting, lenses, and film stock that will work best. Once filming starts, they make adjustments as necessary. They may also film screen tests of actors so the director can be sure they are right for their parts.

Richard Shore, A.S.C., has had a career that extends over 40 years, 20 countries, and 200 films. His feature work includes *Bang the Drum Slowly,* a film that Robert DeNiro credits as starting his career. Currently, Shore is a lecturer at the New York Film Academy (NYFA), where he teaches basic and advanced courses in filmmaking and works one-on-one with students. He teaches classes in cinematography, lighting, scripts, and other aspects of filmmaking.

One of Shore's early filmmaking jobs was making training films for the U.S. Army during the Korean War. "After the war," he says, "I got work making travel films, documentaries, industrial films. I also made TV commercials." This eventually led to a career filled with awards, including two Oscar awards, three Emmy awards, and induction into the American Society of Cinematographers.

Different projects have different demands—for one of the films for which he won an Oscar, a short film about poet Robert Frost, Shore was involved in many aspects of the filmmaking process beyond the duties of DP. For one of the Emmy-winning projects, Shore worked as a director. While working on a documentary about French presi-

And the Oscar Goes To . . .

Want to see the work of some Academy Award-winning cinematographers? Check out the following films:

- Robert Krasker's *The Third Man* (1950)
- Boris Kaufman's *On the Waterfront* (1954)
- Freddie Young's *Doctor Zhivago* (1965)
- Conrad Hall's *Butch Cassidy and the Sundance Kid* (1969)
- Geoffrey Unsworth's *Cabaret* (1972)
- Vilmos Zsigmond's *Close Encounters of the Third Kind* (1977)
- Vittorio Storaro's *The Last Emperor* (1987)
- Peter Biziou's *Mississippi Burning* (1988)
- Janusz Kaminski's *Schindler's List* (1993)
- John Toll's *Braveheart* (1995)
- Peter Pau's *Crouching Tiger, Hidden Dragon* (2000)
- Russell Boy's *Master and Commander: The Far Side of the World* (2003)
- Robert Richardson's *The Aviator* (2004)

For more films by Academy Award–winning cinematographers, visit http://www.oscars.org/awardsdatabase.

dent Francois Mitterand, Shore traveled extensively, spending two months with Mitterand in Paris, then flying with him to Washington, D.C., to meet with President Reagan. "In the film industry," Shore says, "you have experiences you can't get anywhere else."

REQUIREMENTS

High School

You should take courses that will prepare you for college, such as math, English, government, and foreign language. Courses in English composition and literature will give you a background in narrative development, and art and photography courses can help you understand the basics of lighting and composition. A broadcast journalism or media course may give you some hands-on experience in camera operation and video production.

Postsecondary Training

A bachelor's degree in liberal arts or film studies provides a good background for work in the film industry, but practical experience

A cinematographer discusses a shot with a director during an outdoor shoot. *(Photo Disc)*

and industry connections will provide the best job opportunities. Upon completing an undergraduate program, you may wish to enroll in a master's program or master's of fine arts program at a film school. Schools offering well-established programs include the School of Visual Arts in New York, New York University, and the University of Southern California. These schools have film professionals on their faculties and provide a very visible stage for student talent. In addition to classroom time, film school offers students the opportunity to work on their own productions. Such education is rigorous, but in addition to teaching skills it provides you with peer groups and a network of contacts with students, faculty, and guest speakers that can be of help after graduation.

An alternative to film school is the New York Film Academy. NYFA gives students an idea of the demands of filmmaking careers by immersing them in an intensive six-week course. During this time, students have access to cameras and editing tables and are required to make three short films of their own. (Contact information for all schools is listed at the end of this article.)

"A lot of people want to make films," Richard Shore says, "but there is really no direct route to entering the film industry. All production companies care about is what you can show them that you've done. You need to make a short film and submit it to a festival. If it's shown and gets recognition, that's your entrée."

Other Requirements

You'll need to keep abreast of technological innovations while working in the industry. You must be comfortable with the technical as well as artistic aspects of the profession. You also must be a good leader to make decisions and direct your crew effectively.

"You really have to want it," Shore says about the work of a DP. "It's almost like a calling. You can't go into it half-way." Shore says it's also helpful to have your own original story ideas when embarking on a film career. "Film is a storytelling art, a narrative art. Someone with the ideal background is someone interested in literature, particularly the novel."

EXPLORING

With cable television, videos, and DVDs, it is much easier to study films today than it was 25 years ago. It's likely to become even easier as the Internet might someday enable you to download any film you choose. You should take full advantage of the availability of great films and study them closely for different filmmaking styles. The documentary *Visions of Light: The Art of Cinematography,* directed by Arnold Glassman, Todd McCarthy, and Stuart Samuels, is a good introduction to some of the finest cinematography in the history of film. You can also experiment with composition and lighting if you have access to a 16-millimeter camera, a camcorder, or a digital camera. Check with your school's media center or journalism department about recording school events. Your school's drama club can also introduce you to the elements of comedy and drama and may involve you with writing and staging your own productions.

You should subscribe to *American Cinematographer* magazine or read selected articles at the magazine's website (http://www.theasc.com/magazine). Other industry magazines such as *Daily Variety* (http://www.variety.com), *Hollywood Reporter* (http://www.hollywoodreporter.com), and *Cinefex* (http://www.cinefex.com) can also give you insight into filmmaking.

EMPLOYERS

Motion picture studios, production companies, independent producers, and documentary filmmakers all employ DPs, either as salaried employees or as freelancers. The U.S. Department of Labor reports that 20 percent of all camera operators work on a freelance basis. Most freelancers are responsible for finding their own projects to work on, but a few are represented by agents who solicit work for them.

STARTING OUT

Internships are a very good way to gain experience and help you to become a marketable job candidate. Since local television stations and lower-budget film productions operate with limited funds, they may offer internships for course credit or experience instead of a salary. You should check with your state's film commission to learn of productions in your area and volunteer to work in whatever capacity needed. Many production opportunities are also posted on the Web. By working on productions, you'll develop relationships with crew members and production assistants, and you'll be able to build a network of industry connections.

Before working as a DP, you'll likely work as a camera assistant or production assistant. To prepare yourself for this work, try to gain some experience in camera work with a college broadcasting station, a local TV crew, or advertising agency.

Camera operators may choose to join a union because some film studios will hire only union members. The principal union for this field is the International Alliance of Theatrical Stage Employees, Moving Picture Technicians, Artists, and Allied Crafts of the United States, Its Territories and Canada (IATSE). Union members work under a union contract that determines their work rules, pay, and benefits.

ADVANCEMENT

The position of cinematographer is in itself an advanced position. Richard Shore says securing a job as a DP "takes years and years of training. You must work your way up from first assistant, to camera operator, to DP. It's not a union thing, it's a way of learning. You learn from watching cinematographers work."

Those wanting to be DPs must get a foot in the door by making short films and getting them seen by producers. "Not only do you need skills, but you must make connections with people," Shore explains.

Camera operators may have opportunities to work as cinematographers on some projects. As they continue to develop relationships with filmmakers and producers, their DP work may increase, leading to better-paying, high-profile film projects. Once a DP has begun working in the industry, advancement may come as the DP develops a reputation for excellent, innovative work. Directors and producers may then request to work with that particular DP, which can also lead to higher pay.

EARNINGS

Many DPs do freelance work or have jobs under union contracts. They may work for a variety of employers ranging from major studios producing films with multimillion-dollar budgets to small, independent producers who are financing a film with their credit cards. As a result, their earnings vary widely.

When starting out as a camera operator, an individual may volunteer for a job, without pay, simply to get experience. At the other end of the earnings scale, a well-established DP working on big-budget productions can make well over a million dollars a year. The IATSE establishes minimum wage scales for DPs who are union members, based on the nature of a film shoot. In 2003, for feature film studio shoots, a cinematographer was paid about $520 a day. For location shoots, the wage was about $670 a day. Special provisions for holiday and overtime work are also made.

For an idea of what the average cinematographer may make in a year, consider government findings. The U.S. Department of Labor reports that mean annual earnings for DPs working in the motion picture and video industries were $50,590 in 2004. Camera operators who were employed in the motion picture, television, and video industries earned salaries that ranged from less than $15,730 to more than $76,100.

Freelancers must pay for their own benefits, such as health insurance, and they usually must buy their own equipment, which can be quite expensive.

WORK ENVIRONMENT

Conditions of work will vary depending on the size and nature of the production. In television production and in movies, DPs may work both indoors and outdoors. Indoors, conditions can be cramped, while outdoors there may be heat, cold, rain, or snow. DPs may need to travel for weeks at a time while a project is being shot on location, and some locations, such as the middle of a desert, may mean staying miles from civilization. Hours can be long and the shooting schedule rigorous, especially when a film is going over budget. DPs work as members of a team, instructing assistants while also taking instruction from directors and producers. Those making a film with a small budget may be required to oversee many different aspects of the production.

Filming challenges, such as how to shoot effectively underwater, in the dark, or in public areas, are a normal part of the job. DPs need patience in setting up cameras and preparing the lighting, as well as in dealing with the variety of professionals with whom they work.

"If you can get into film," Richard Shore says, "it's a wonderful career." One reason DPs enjoy their work so much is that they work with talented, artistic, and skillful professionals. "There's a camaraderie among film crew members," Shore says.

OUTLOOK

The U.S. Department of Labor predicts employment for camera operators to grow faster than the average through 2012. More opportunities, though, will be available for those willing to work outside of the film industry at, for example, advertising agencies and TV broadcasting companies. The department anticipates that other types of programming, such as Internet broadcasts of music videos, sports, and general information shows, will provide job openings in this field.

However, competition for work will be fierce because so many people are attracted to this business. "There are so many more qualified people than there are jobs," Richard Shore says. "It's impossible to guarantee success." Nevertheless, those with the right connections, strong samples of their work, and some luck are likely to find opportunities.

DPs of the future will be working more closely with special effects houses, even on films other than science fiction, horror, and other genres typically associated with special effects. Digital technology is used to create crowd scenes, underwater images, and other effects more efficiently and economically. DPs will have to approach a film with an understanding of which shots can be produced digitally and which will require traditional methods of filmmaking.

FOR MORE INFORMATION

For information about education and training workshops for television and film production and to read about events in the industry, visit the AFI website.
American Film Institute (AFI)
2021 North Western Avenue
Los Angeles, CA 90027-1657
Tel: 323-856-7600
http://www.afi.com

This website has information on the ASC, articles from American Cinematographer *magazine, industry news, and a students' section with grants and fellowship information. The ASC online store sells many helpful publications covering aspects of film production.*

American Society of Cinematographers (ASC)
PO Box 2230
Hollywood, CA 90078
Tel: 800-448-0145
Email: info@theasc.com
http://theasc.com

For information on membership benefits, contact this branch of the International Alliance of Theatrical Stage Employees (IATSE).

International Cinematographers Guild (IATSE Local 600)
National Office/Western Region
7755 Sunset Boulevard, Suite 300
Hollywood, CA 90046
Tel: 323-876-0160
http://www.cameraguild.com

Visit this website organized by the ASC for a list of film schools and to learn about the career of cinematographer—the next step on the career ladder for camera operators.

Cinematographer.com
http://www.cinematographer.com

To read about film programs at several schools, visit the following websites:

New York Film Academy
http://www.nyfa.com

New York University
http://www.nyu.edu

School of Visual Arts
http://schoolofvisualarts.edu

University of Southern California
http://www.usc.edu

Composers and Arrangers

QUICK FACTS

School Subjects
Music
Theater/dance

Personal Skills
Artistic
Communication/ideas

Work Environment
Primarily indoors
Primarily one location

Minimum Education Level
High school diploma

Salary Range
$15,960 to $75,940 to
$100,000+

Certification or Licensing
None available

Outlook
About as fast as the average

DOT
152

GOE
01.04.02

NOC
5132

O*NET-SOC
27-2041.02, 27-2041.03

OVERVIEW

Composers create much of the music heard every day on radio and television, in films, in theaters and concert halls, on recordings and in advertising, and through any other medium of musical presentation. Composers write symphonies, concertos, and operas; scores for theater, television, and cinema; and music for musical theater, recording artists, and commercial advertising. They may combine elements of classical music with elements of popular musical styles such as rock, jazz, reggae, folk, and others. *Arrangers* take composers' musical compositions and transcribe them for other instruments or voices; work them into scores for film, theater, or television; or adapt them to styles that are different from the one in which the music was written.

HISTORY

Classical (used in the widest sense) composition probably dates back to the late Middle Ages, when musical notation began to develop in Christian monasteries. In those times and for some centuries thereafter, the church was the main patron of musical composition. During the 14th century, or possibly earlier, the writing of music in score (that is, for several instruments or instruments and voices) began to take place. This was the beginning of orchestral writing. Composers then were mostly sponsored by the church and were supposed to be religiously motivated in their work, which was not to be considered an expression of their own emotions. It was probably not until the end of the 15th century that the work of a composer began to be recognized as a statement of individual expression. Recognition of composers did not really become common until several centuries later. Even Johann Sebastian Bach, writing in the 18th century, was known more as an organist and choirmaster during his lifetime.

The writing of music in score was the beginning of a great change in the history of music. The craft of making musical instruments and the techniques of playing them were advancing also. By the beginning of the Baroque Period, around 1600, these changes brought musical composition to a new stage of development, which was enhanced by patronage from secular sources. The nobility had taken an interest in sponsoring musical composition, and over the next two to three hundred years they came to supplant the church as the main patrons of composers. Under their patronage, composers had more room to experiment and develop new musical styles.

During the Baroque Period, which lasted until about 1750, there was a flowering of musical forms, including opera. In the early 1600s, Rome became preeminent in opera, using the chorus and dance to embellish the operatic spectacle. Instrumental music also grew during this period, reaching its greatest flowering in the work of Johann Sebastian Bach and George Frederick Handel. The major musical forms of Baroque origin were the sonata and cantata, both largely attributed to the composers of opera.

The "true" Classical Period in music began in about the mid-18th century and lasted through the 19th century. Composers embellishing the sonata form now developed the symphony. Through the latter half of the 19th century, most composers of symphonies, concerti, chamber music, and other instrumental forms adhered to the strict formality of the Classical tradition. In the 19th century, however, many composers broke from Classical formalism, instilling greater emotionalism, subjectivity, and individualism in their work. The new musical style evolved into what became formally known as the Romantic movement in music. Romanticism did not replace classicism, but rather, it existed side by side with the older form. A transitional figure in the break from classicism was Ludwig van Beethoven, whose compositions elevated the symphonic form to its highest level. Other composers who perfected the Romantic style included Franz Schubert, Franz Liszt, Johannes Brahms, Hector Berlioz, and Peter Ilich Tchaikovsky in orchestral music, and Giuseppe Verdi and Richard Wagner in opera.

Many of the composers of the early Classical Period labored for little more than recognition. Their monetary rewards were often meager. In the 19th century, however, as the stature of the composers grew, they were able to gain more control over their own work and the proceeds that it produced. The opera composers, in particular, were able to reap quite handsome profits.

Another abrupt break from tradition occurred at the beginning of the 20th century. At that time composers began to turn away from Romanticism and seek new and original styles and sounds. Audiences sometimes were repulsed by these new musical sounds, but eventually they were accepted and imitated by other composers. One of the most successful of the post-Romantic composers was Igor Stravinsky, whose landmark work *The Rite of Spring* was hailed by some to be the greatest work of the century.

Through the 20th century composers continued to write music in the styles of the past and to experiment with new styles. Some contemporary composers, such as George Gershwin and Leonard Bernstein, wrote for both popular and serious audiences. John Cage, Philip Glass, Steve Reich, and other composers moved even further from traditional forms and musical instruments, experimenting with electronically created music, in which an electronic instrument, such as a synthesizer, is used to compose and play music. An even more significant advance is the use of computers as a compositional tool. In the 21st century, the only thing predictable in musical composition is that experimentation and change are certain to continue.

THE JOB

Composers express themselves in music much as writers express themselves with words and painters with line, shape, and color. Although influenced by what they hear, composers' compositions are original because they reflect their own interpretation and use of musical elements. All composers use the same basic musical elements, including harmony, melody, counterpoint, and rhythm, but each composer applies these elements in a unique way. Music schools teach all of the elements that go into composition, providing composers with the tools needed for their work, but how a composer uses these tools to create music is what sets an individual apart.

There is no prescribed way for a composer to go about composing. All composers work in a somewhat different way, but generally speaking they pursue their work in some kind of regular, patterned way, in much the same fashion of a novelist or a painter. Composers may work in different areas of classical music, writing, for example, symphonies, operas, concerti, music for a specific instrument or grouping of instruments, and for voice. Many composers also work

Top Film Scores

The following film scores (listed in alphabetical order) are widely considered to be among the best of the last four decades:

American Beauty, by Thomas Newman (1999)

Batman, by Danny Elfman (1989)

Close Encounters of the Third Kind, by John Williams (1977)

Dances With Wolves, by John Barry (1990)

Edward Scissorhands, by Danny Elfman (1990)

The Empire Strikes Back, by John Williams (1980)

E.T., by John Williams (1982)

Glory, by James Horner (1989)

Jaws, by John Williams (1975)

The Mission, by Ennio Morricone (1986)

Out of Africa, by John Barry/Mozart (1985)

Poltergeist, by Jerry Goldsmith (1982)

Raiders of the Lost Ark, by John Williams (1981)

Schindler's List, by John Williams (1993)

Taxi Driver, by Bernard Herrmann (1975)

in popular music and incorporate popular music ideas in their classical compositions.

Composers may create compositions out of sheer inspiration, with or without a particular market in mind, or they may be commissioned to write a piece of music for a particular purpose. Composers who write music on their own then have the problem of finding someone to perform their music in the hopes that it will be well received and lead to further performances and possibly a recording. The more a composer's music is played and recorded, the greater the chances to sell future offerings and to receive commissions for new work. Commissions come from institutions (where the composer may or may not be a faculty member), societies and associations, orchestral groups, or from film, television, and commercial projects. Almost every film has a score, the music playing throughout the film apart from any songs that may also be in the film.

A composer who wishes to make a living by writing music should understand the musical marketplace as well as possible. It should be understood that only a small percentage of music composers can make their living solely by writing music. To make a dent in the marketplace one should be familiar with its major components:

Film and television. There is a very large market for original compositions in feature and industrial films, television programs, and videos. The industry is in constant need of original scores and thematic music.

Performance. Composers usually rely on one of two ways to have their music performed: they contact musical performers or producers who are most likely to be receptive to their style of composition, or they may write for a musical group in which they are performers.

Music publishing. Music publishers seek composers who are talented and whose work they feel it will be profitable to promote. They take a cut of the royalties, but they relieve composers of all of the business and legal detail of their profession. Composers today have rather commonly turned to self-publishing.

Copying. A musical composition written for several pieces or voices requires copying into various parts. Composers may do this work themselves, but it is an exacting task for which professional copiers may be employed. Many composers themselves take on copying work as a sideline.

Computerization. Computers have become an increasingly important tool for composing and copying. Some composers have set up incredibly sophisticated computerized studios in which they compose, score, and play an orchestrated piece by computer. They can also do the copying and produce a recording. Perhaps the most significant enhancement to the home studio is the Musical Instrument Digital Interface, which transposes the composer's work into computer language and then converts it into notation.

Recording. Knowing the recording industry is an important aspect in advancing a composer's career. An unrecognized composer will find it difficult to catch on with a commercial recording company, but it is not uncommon for a composer to make his own recording and handle the distribution and promotion as well.

Students interested in composing can tap into any number of organizations and associations for more detail on any area of musical composition. One such organization providing support and information is Meet the Composer, which is headquartered in New York and has several national affiliates.

Arrangers generally create a musical background for a preexisting melody. An arranger may create an introduction and a coda (ending) for a melody as well as add countermelodies (additional melodies) to the original melody. In effect, the arranger composes additional material that was not provided by the original composer and ensures that the original melody is set off by its background in an effective manner. Most arrangers are musicians themselves and have an excellent knowledge of musical styles and current trends.

An *orchestrator* takes a piece of music, perhaps one that already has a basic arrangement, and assigns the parts to specific instruments in the orchestra or other ensemble. For this reason, the orchestrator must have a tremendous amount of knowledge regarding exactly what the various instruments can and cannot do. An orchestrator may decide, for example, that a particular melody should be played by a solo flute or by a flute and an oboe, so that a very specific sound will be achieved. An orchestrator must also know how to notate parts for various instruments. All the choices that the orchestrator makes will have a significant impact on the way the music will sound. Arranging and orchestrating are very closely related, and many professionals perform both tasks. Many composers also do their own arranging and orchestrating.

REQUIREMENTS

High School

There is no specific course of training that will help you to become a composer. Many composers begin composing from a very early age and receive tutoring and training to encourage their talent. Musically inclined students should continue their private studies and take advantage of everything musical their high school offers. If you are interested in creating music for motion pictures and television, you should listen to as many scores from these sources as possible. Specially gifted students usually find their way to schools or academies that specialize in music or the arts. These students may begin learning composition in this special environment, and some might begin to create original compositions.

Postsecondary Training

After high school, you can continue your education in any of numerous colleges and universities or special music schools or conservatories that offer bachelor's and higher degrees. Your course of study will include music history, music criticism, music theory, harmony, counterpoint, rhythm, melody, and ear training. In most major music schools courses in composition are offered along with orchestration and arranging. Courses are also taught covering voice and the major musical instruments, including keyboard, guitar, and, more recently, synthesizer. Most schools now cover computer techniques as applied to music as well. It may also be helpful to learn at least one foreign language; German, French, and Italian are good choices.

Other Requirements

None of this is to say that study in a musical institution is required for a composer or is any guarantee of success. Some say that composing cannot be taught, that the combination of skills, talent, and inspiration required to create music is a highly individual occurrence. Authorities have argued on both sides of this issue without resolution. It does appear that genetics plays a strong part in musical ability; musical people often come from musical families. There are many contradictions of this, however, and some authorities cite the musical environment as being highly influential. The great composers were extraordinarily gifted, and it is very possible that achieving even moderate success in music requires special talent. Nevertheless, you will not be successful unless you work extremely hard and remain dedicated to improving your compositional talents at every opportunity. Prospective composers are also advised to become proficient on at least one instrument.

EXPLORING

Musical programs offered by local schools, YMCAs, and community centers offer good beginning opportunities. It is especially helpful to learn to play a musical instrument, such as the piano, violin, or cello. Attending concerts and recitals and reading about music and musicians and their careers will also provide you with good background and experience. There are also any number of videos available through your school or local library that will teach you about music. You should also form or join musical groups and attempt to write music for your group to perform. There are also many books that provide good reference information on careers in composing and arranging. If you are interested in writing scores for films, check out a copy of *Film Score Monthly* (http://www.filmscoremonthly.com), which features useful articles and resources for film composers. The magazine also offers a useful article on becoming a composer—it can be accessed by visiting http://www.filmscor emonthly.com/features/beacomposer.asp. *Film Music* magazine (http://www.filmmusicmag.com) is another comprehensive resource for aspiring and professional film composers.

EMPLOYERS

Composers are self-employed. They complete their work in their own studios and then try to sell their pieces to music publishers, film and television production companies, or recording companies. Once their work becomes well known, clients, such as film and television producers, dance companies, or musical theater producers, may commission original pieces from composers. In this case, the client provides a story line, time period, mood, and other specifications the composer must honor in the creation of a musical score.

Advertising agencies and studios that make commercials and film, television, and video production studios might have a few "house" composers on staff. Schools often underwrite a composer in residence, and many composers work as professors in college and university music departments while continuing to compose. For the most part, however, composers are on their own to create and promote their work.

Most arrangers work on a freelance basis for record companies, musical artists, music publishers, and film and television production companies.

STARTING OUT

In school, young composers should try to have their work performed either at school concerts or by local school or community ensembles. This will also most likely involve the composers in copying and scoring their work and possibly even directing. Student film projects can provide an opportunity for experience at film composing and scoring. Working in school or local musical theater companies can provide valuable experience. Personal connections made in these projects may be very helpful in the professional world that lies ahead. Developing a portfolio of work will be helpful as the composer enters a professional career.

Producers of public service announcements, or PSAs, for radio and television are frequently on the lookout for pro bono (volunteer) work that can provide opportunities for young, willing composers. Such opportunities may be listed in trade magazines, such as *Variety* (http://www.variety.com) and *Show Business* (http://showbusinessweekly.com).

Joining the American Federation of Musicians and other musical societies and associations is another good move for aspiring composers. Among the associations that can be contacted are Meet the Composer, the American Composers Alliance, Broadcast Music Inc.,

Useful Websites for Film Composers

Film Music Society
http://www.filmmusicsociety.org

Film Music Magazine
http://www.filmmusicmag.com

Film Score Monthly
http://www.filmscoremonthly.com

So You Want to be a Film Composer (from *Film Score Monthly*)
http://www.filmscoremonthly.com/features/beacomposer.asp

Soundtrack.net
http://www.soundtrack.net

the Society of Composers, and the American Society of Composers, Authors, and Publishers (ASCAP), all located in New York. These associations and the trade papers are also good sources for leads on grants and awards for which composers can apply.

Young composers, arrangers, songwriters, and jingle writers can also work their way into the commercial advertising business by doing some research and taking entry-level jobs with agencies that handle musical commercials.

ADVANCEMENT

Moving ahead in the music world is done strictly on an individual basis. There is no hierarchical structure to climb, although in record companies a person with music writing talent might move into a producing or A&R (Artist & Repertoire) job and be able to exercise compositional skills in those capacities. Advancement is based on talent, determination, and, probably, luck. Some composers become well known for their work with film scores; John Williams, of *Star Wars* fame, is one.

Advancement for composers and arrangers often takes place on a highly personal level. They may progress through their careers to writing or transcribing music of greater complexity and in more challenging structures. They may develop a unique style and even develop new forms and traditions of music. One day, their names might be added to the list of the great composers and arrangers.

EARNINGS

A few composers make huge annual incomes, while many make little or nothing. Some make a very large income in one or two years and none in succeeding years. While many composers receive royalties on repeat performances of their work, most depend on commissions to support themselves. Commissions vary widely according to the type of work and the industry for which the work will be performed. Music directors, composers, and arrangers employed in the motion picture and video industries had mean annual earnings of $75,940, according to the U.S. Department of Labor. Salaries for all music directors, composers, and arrangers ranged from less than $15,960 to more than $75,380. Well-known composers and arrangers can earn salaries that exceed $100,000 a year.

Many composers, however, do not hold full-time salaried positions and are only paid in royalties for their compositions that sell. According to the ASCAP, the royalty rate for 2004 was $.085 per song per album sold. The $.085 is divided between the composer and the publisher, based on their agreement. If the album sold 25,000 copies in 2004, the royalties the composer and publisher received would be $2,125. Naturally, if this song is the only one the composer has that brings in income during this time, his or her annual earnings are extremely low (keep in mind that the composer receives only a percentage of the $2,125).

On the other hand, a composer who creates music for a feature film may have substantial earnings, according to the ASCAP. Factors that influence the composer's earnings include how much music is needed for the film, the film's total budget, if the film will be distributed to a general audience or have only limited showings, and the reputation of the composer. The ASCAP notes that depending on such factors, a composer can receive fees ranging from $20,000 for a lower budget, small film to more than $1,000,000 if the film is a big budget release from a major studio and the composer is well known.

Many composers and arrangers must hold a second job in order to make ends meet financially. In some cases these second jobs, such as teaching, will provide benefits such as health insurance and paid vacation time. Composers and arrangers who work independently, however, need to provide insurance and other benefits for themselves.

WORK ENVIRONMENT

The physical conditions of a composer's workplace can vary according to personal taste and what is affordable. Some work in expensive, state-of-the-art home studios, others in a bare room with an electric keyboard or a guitar. An aspiring composer may work in a cramped and cluttered room in a New York City tenement or in a Hollywood ranch home.

For the serious composer the work is likely to be personally rewarding but financially unrewarding. For the commercial writer, some degree of financial reward is more likely, but competition is fierce, and top earnings go only to the rarest of individuals. Getting started requires great dedication and sacrifice. Even those protected by academia must give up most of their spare time to composing, often sitting down to the piano when exhausted from a full day of teaching. There are many frustrations along the way. The career composer must learn to live with rejection and have the verve and determination to keep coming back time and again. Under these circumstances, composers can only succeed by having complete faith in their own work.

OUTLOOK

The U.S. Department of Labor, which classifies composers and arrangers in the category of musicians, singers, and related workers, predicts employment in this field to grow about as fast as the average through 2012. Although there are no reliable statistics on the number of people who make their living solely from composing and/or arranging, the general consensus is that very few people can sustain themselves through composing and arranging alone. The field is highly competitive and crowded with highly talented people trying to have their music published and played. There are only a limited number of commissions, grants, and awards available at any time, and the availability of these is often subjected to changes in the economy. On the other hand, many films continue to be made each year, particularly as cable television companies produce more and more original programs. However, the chances of new composers and arrangers supporting themselves by their music alone will likely always remain small.

FOR MORE INFORMATION

For profiles of composers of concert music, visit the ACA website.
   American Composers Alliance (ACA)
   648 Broadway, Room 803
   New York, NY 10012
   Tel: 212-362-8900

Email: info@composers.com
http://www.composers.com

For professional and artistic development resources, contact
American Composers Forum
332 Minnesota Street, Suite East 145
St. Paul, MN 55101-1300
Tel: 651-228-1407
http://www.composersforum.org

*For music news, news on legislation affecting musicians, and the
magazine* International Musician, *contact*
**American Federation of Musicians of the United States and
    Canada**
1501 Broadway, Suite 600
New York, NY 10036
Tel: 212-869-1330
Email: info@afm.org
http://www.afm.org

*For articles on songwriting, information on workshops and awards,
and practical information about the business of music, contact*
American Society of Composers, Authors, and Publishers
One Lincoln Plaza
New York, NY 10023
Tel: 212-621-6000
Email: info@ascap.com
http://www.ascap.com

*This organization represents songwriters, composers, and music pub-
lishers. Its website has useful information on the industry.*
Broadcast Music Inc.
320 West 57th Street
New York, NY 10019-3790
Tel: 212-586-2000
http://www.bmi.com

*This organization "promotes the preservation of film and television
music." Visit its website for more information.*
Film Music Society
15125 Ventura Boulevard, Suite 201
Sherman Oaks, CA 91403
Tel: 818-789-6404

Email: info@filmmusicsociety.org
http://www.filmmusicsociety.org

The IAWM website has information for and about women composers.
International Alliance for Women in Music (IAWM)
Rollins College
1000 Holt Avenue, Box 2731
Winter Park, FL 32789-4499
Email: slackman@rollins.edu
http://www.iawm.org

The Meet the Composer website has information on awards and residencies as well as interviews with composers active in the field today.
Meet the Composer
75 Ninth Avenue, 3R Suite C
New York, NY 10011
Tel: 212-645-6949
http://www.meetthecomposer.org

For information on student membership and commission competitions, contact
Society of Composers
Box 450
New York, NY 10113-0450
http://www.societyofcomposers.org

Visit the following website to view a registry of film and television composers.
http://www.soundtrack.net/composers

Costume Designers

OVERVIEW

Costume designers plan, create, and maintain clothing and accessories for all characters in a stage, film, television, dance, or opera production. Designers custom fit each character, and either create a new garment or alter an existing costume.

HISTORY

Costume design has been an important part of the theater since the early Greek tragedies, when actors generally wore masks and long robes with sleeves. By the time of the Roman Caesars, stage costumes had become very elaborate and colorful.

After the fall of Rome, theater disappeared for some time, but later returned in the form of Easter and Nativity plays. Priests and choirboys wore their usual robes with some simple additions, such as veils and crowns. Plays then moved from the church to the marketplace, and costumes again became important to the production.

During the Renaissance, costumes were designed for the Italian pageants, the French ballets, and the English masques by such famous designers as Torelli, Jean Berain, and Burnacini. From 1760 to 1782, Louis-Rene Boquet designed costumes using wide panniers, forming a kind of elaborate ballet skirt. But by the end of the 18th century, there was a movement toward more classical costumes on the stage.

During the early 19th century, historical costumes became popular, and period details were added to contemporary dress. Toward the end of the 19th century, realism became important, and actors wore the dress of the day, often their own clothes. Because this trend result-ed in less work for the costume designers, they turned to musical and opera productions to express their creativity.

In the early 20th century, Diaghilev's Russian Ballet introduced a non-naturalistic style in costumes, most notably in the designs of Leon Bakst. This trend gave way to European avant-garde theater, in which costumes became abstract and symbolic.

Since the 1960s, new materials, such as plastics and adhesives, have greatly increased the costume designer's range. Today, their work is prominent in plays, musicals, dance performances, films, music videos, and television programs.

THE JOB

Costume designers generally work as freelancers. After they have been contracted to provide the costumes for a production, they read the script to learn about the theme, location, time period, character types, dialogue, and action. They meet with the director to discuss his or her feelings on the plot, characters, period and style, time frame for the production, and budget.

For a play, designers plan a rough costume plot, which is a list of costume changes by scene for each character. They thoroughly research the history and setting in which the play is set. They plan a preliminary color scheme and sketch the costumes, including details such as gloves, footwear, hose, purses, jewelry, canes, fans, bouquets, and other props. The costume designer or an assistant collects swatch-es of fabrics and samples of various accessories.

After completing the research, final color sketches are painted or drawn and mounted for presentation. Once the director approves the designs, the costume designer solicits bids from contractors, creates or rents costumes, and shops for fabrics and accessories. Measurements of all actors are taken. Designers work closely with drapers, sewers, hairstylists, and makeup artists in the costume shop. They supervise fittings and attend all dress rehearsals to make final adjustments and repairs.

Costume designers also work in films, television, and videos, aim-ing to provide the look that will highlight characters' personalities. Aside from working with actors, they may also design and create cos-tumes for performers such as figure skaters, ballroom dance com-petitors, circus members, theme park characters, rock artists, and others who routinely wear costumes as part of a show.

REQUIREMENTS
High School
Costume designers need at least a high school education. It is helpful to take classes in art, home economics, and theater and to participate in drama clubs or community theater. English, literature, and history classes will help you learn how to analyze a play and research the clothing and manner of various historical periods. Marketing and business-related classes will also be helpful, as most costume designers work as freelancers. Familiarity with computers is useful, as many designers work with computer-aided design (CAD) programs.

While in high school, consider starting a portfolio of design sketches. Practicing in a sketchbook is a great way to get ideas and designs out on paper and organized for future reference. You can also get design ideas through others; watch theater, television, or movie productions and take note of the characters' dress. Sketch them on your own for practice. Looking through fashion magazines can also give you ideas to sketch.

Postsecondary Training
A college degree is not a requirement, but in this highly competitive field, it gives a sizable advantage. Most costume designers today have a bachelor's degree. Many art schools, especially in New York and Los Angeles, have programs in costume design at both the bachelor's and master's degree level. A liberal arts school with a strong theater program is also a good choice.

Other Requirements
Costume designers need sewing, draping, and patterning skills, as well as training in basic design techniques and figure drawing. Aside from being artistic, designers must also be able to work with people because many compromises and agreements must be made between the designer and the production's director.

Costume designers must prepare a portfolio of their work, including photographs and sketches highlighting their best efforts. Some theatrical organizations require membership in United Scenic Artists (USA), a union that protects the interests of designers on the job and sets minimum fees. Students in design programs that pass an exam and have some design experience can apply for USA's Designer Apprentice Program. More experienced designers who want full professional membership in the union must also submit a portfolio for review.

EXPLORING

If you are interested in costume design, consider joining a theater organization, such as a school drama club or a community theater. School dance troupes or film classes also may offer opportunities to explore costume design.

The Costume Designer's Handbook: A Complete Guide for Amateur and Professional Costume Designers, by Rosemary Ingham and Liz Covey (Portsmouth, N.H.: Heinemann, 1992), is an invaluable resource for beginning or experienced costume designers.

You can practice designing on your own, by drawing original sketches or copying designs from television, films, or the stage. Practice sewing and altering costumes from sketches for yourself, friends, and family.

EMPLOYERS

Costume designers are employed by production companies that produce works for stage, television, and film. Most employers are located in New York and Los Angeles, although most metropolitan areas have community theater and film production companies that hire designers.

STARTING OUT

Most high schools and colleges have drama clubs and dance groups that need costumes designed and made. Community theaters, too, may offer opportunities to assist in costume production. Regional theaters hire several hundred costume technicians each year for seasons that vary from 28 to 50 weeks.

Many beginning designers enter the field by becoming an assistant to a designer. Many established designers welcome newcomers and can be generous mentors. Some beginning workers start out in costume shops, which usually requires membership in a union. However, nonunion workers may be allowed to work for short-term projects. Some designers begin as *shoppers*, who swatch fabrics, compare prices, and buy yardage, trim, and accessories. Shoppers learn where to find the best materials at reasonable prices and often establish valuable contacts in the field. Other starting positions include milliner's assistant, craft assistant, or assistant to the draper.

Schools with bachelor's and master's programs in costume design may offer internships that can lead to jobs after graduation. Another method of entering costume design is to contact regional theaters directly and send your resume to the theater's managing director.

Before you become a costume designer, you may want to work as a freelance design assistant for a few years to gain helpful experience, a reputation, contacts, and an impressive portfolio.

ADVANCEMENT

Beginning designers must show they are willing to do a variety of tasks. The theater community is small and intricately interconnected, so those who work hard and are flexible with assignments can gain good reputations quickly. Smaller regional theaters tend to hire designers for a full season to work with the same people on one or more productions, so opportunities for movement may be scarce. Eventually, costume designers with experience and talent can work for larger productions, such as films, television, and videos.

EARNINGS

Earnings vary greatly in this business depending on factors such as how many outfits the designer completes, how long they are employed during the year, and the amount of their experience. Although the U.S. Department of Labor does not give salary figures for costume designers, it does report that the related occupational group of costume attendants had a median hourly wage of $12.04 in 2004. For full-time work, this hourly wage translates into a yearly income of approximately $25,050. However, those just starting out and working as assistants earned as little as $7.18 an hour, translating into an annual salary of approximately $14,930. Experienced costume attendants can earn $23.28 or more per hour (or an annual salary of $48,430 or more).

Costume designers who work on Broadway or for other large stage productions are usually members of the United Scenic Artists union, which sets minimum fees, requires producers to pay into pension and welfare funds, protects the designer's rights, establishes rules for billing, and offers group health and life insurance.

According to the union, a costume designer for a Broadway musical with a minimum of 36 actors earns around $30,900. For a Broadway drama with a minimum of 36 actors, a costume designer earns a minimum of approximately $14,580. For opera and dance companies, salary is usually by costume count.

For feature films and television, costume designers earn daily rates for an eight-hour day or a weekly rate for an unlimited number of hours. Designers sometimes earn royalties on their designs.

Regional theaters usually set individual standard fees, which vary widely, beginning around $200 per week for an assistant. Most of them do not require membership in the union.

Most costume designers work freelance and are paid per costume or show. Costume designers can charge $90 to $500 per costume, but some costumes, such as those for figure skaters, can cost thousands of dollars. Freelance costume designers often receive a flat rate for designing costumes for a show. For small and regional theaters, this rate may be in the $400 to $500 range; the flat rate for medium and large productions generally starts at around $1,000. Many costume designers must take second part-time or full-time jobs to supplement their income from costume design.

Freelancers are responsible for their own health insurance, life insurance, and pension plans. They do not receive holiday, sick, or vacation pay.

WORK ENVIRONMENT

Costume designers put in long hours at painstaking detail work. It is a demanding profession that requires flexible, artistic, and practical workers. The schedule can be erratic—a busy period followed by weeks of little or no work. Though costumes are often a crucial part of a production's success, designers usually get little recognition compared to the actors and director.

Designers meet a variety of interesting and gifted people. Every play, film, or concert is different and every production situation is unique, so there is rarely a steady routine. Costume designers must play many roles: artist, sewer, researcher, buyer, manager, and negotiator.

OUTLOOK

The U.S. Department of Labor predicts employment for tailors, dressmakers, and skilled sewers to decline through 2012, and costume designers may not fair much better. The health of the entertainment business, especially theater, is very dependent on the overall economy and public attitudes. Theater budgets and government support for the arts in general have come under pressure in recent years and have limited employment prospects for costume designers. Many theaters, especially small and nonprofit theaters, are cutting their budgets or doing smaller shows that require fewer costumes. Additionally, people are less willing to spend money on tickets or go to theaters during economic downturns or times of crisis.

Nevertheless, opportunities for costume designers exist. As more cable television networks create original programming, demand for costume design in this area is likely to increase. Costume designers are able to work in an increasing number of locations as new regional theaters and cable television companies operate throughout the United States. As a result, however, designers must be willing to travel.

Competition for designer jobs is stiff and will remain so throughout the next decade. The number of qualified costume designers far exceeds the number of jobs available. This is especially true in smaller cities and regions, where there are fewer theaters.

FOR MORE INFORMATION

This union represents costume designers in film and television. For information on the industry, to read career information, and to view costume sketches in its online gallery, check out the Guild's website.

Costume Designers Guild
4730 Woodman Avenue, Suite 430
Sherman Oaks, CA 91423
Tel: 818-905-1557
Email: cdgia@earthlink.net
http://www.costumedesignersguild.com

This organization provides a list of schools, scholarships, and a journal. College memberships are available with opportunities to network among other members who are professionals in the costume field.

Costume Society of America
PO Box 73
Earleville, MD 21919
Tel: 800-272-9447
Email: national.office@costumesocietyamerica.com
http://www.costumesocietyamerica.com

For additional information, contact the following organizations.

National Costumers Association
121 North Bosart Avenue
Indianapolis, IN 46201
Tel: 317-351-1940
Email: office@costumers.org
http://www.costumers.org

United States Institute for Theatre Technology
6443 Ridings Road
Syracuse, NY 13206-1111
Tel: 800-938-7488
Email: info@office.usitt.org
http://www.usitt.org

This union represents many costume designers working in New York, Chicago, Los Angeles, Miami, and New England. For information on membership, apprenticeship programs, and other resources on the career, contact
United Scenic Artists Local 829
29 West 38th Street
New York, NY 10018
Tel: 212-581-0300
http://www.usa829.org

Film Directors

OVERVIEW

"Lights! Camera! Action!" aptly summarizes the major responsibilities of the *film director*. In ultimate control of the decisions that shape a film production, the director is an artist who coordinates the elements of a film and is responsible for its overall style and quality.

Directors are well known for their part in guiding actors, but they are involved in much more—casting, costuming, cinematography, editing, and sound recording. Directors must have insight into the many tasks that go into the creation of a film, and they must have a broad vision of how each part will contribute to the big picture.

HISTORY

The playwrights and actors of ancient Greece were tellers of tales, striving to impress and influence audiences with their dramatic interpretations of stories. That tradition continues today on stages and film screens throughout the world.

From the days of the Greek theater until sometime in the 19th century, actors directed themselves. Although modern motion picture directors can find their roots in the theater, it was not until the mid-1880s that the director became someone other than a member of the acting cast. It had been common practice for one of the actors involved in a production to be responsible not only for his or her own performance but also for conducting rehearsals and coordinating the tasks involved in putting on a play. Usually the most experienced and respected troupe member would guide the other actors, providing advice on speech, movement, and interaction.

A British actress and opera singer named Madame Vestris is considered to have been the first professional director. In the 1830s Vestris leased a theater in London and staged productions in which she herself did not perform. She displayed a new, creative approach to directing, making bold decisions about changing the traditional dress code for actors and allowing them to express their own interpretations of their roles. Vestris coordinated rehearsals, advised on lighting and sound effects, and chose nontraditional set decorations; she introduced props, such as actual windows and doors, that were more realistic than the usual painted panoramas.

By the turn of the century, theater directors such as David Belasco and Konstantin Stanislavsky had influenced the way in which performances were given, provoking actors and actresses to strive to identify with the characters they revealed so that audiences would be passionately and genuinely affected. By the early 1900s, Stanislavsky's method of directing performers had made an overwhelming mark on drama. His method (now often referred to as "the Method"), as well as his famous criticism, "I do not believe you," continues to influence performers to this day.

At this same time, the motion picture industry was coming into being. European filmmakers such as Leon Gaumont and New Yorker Edwin S. Porter were directing, filming, and producing short pictures. The industry's first professional female director was Alice Guy, who worked with Gaumont in the early years of the 20th century. The technical sophistication offered by today's professionals was not part of the early directors' repertoire. They merely filmed narratives without moving their camera. Soon directors began to experiment, moving the camera to shoot various angles and establishing a variety of editing techniques.

By 1915, there were close to 20,000 movie theaters in the United States; by the early 1920s, 40 million people were going to Hollywood-produced and -directed silent movies every week. Successful actors such as Charlie Chaplin and Buster Keaton began directing their own films, and Frank Capra and Cecil B. De Mille were starting their long careers as professional directors.

With the emergence of "talking pictures" in the early 1930s, the director's role changed significantly. Sound in film provided opportunities for further directorial creativity. Unnecessary noise could not be tolerated on the set; directors had to be concerned with the voices of their performers and the potential sound effects that could be created. Directors could demand certain types of voices (e.g., a Southern drawl) and sound effects (e.g., the rat-a-tat-tat of submachine guns) to present accurate interpretations of scripts. And no

A director studies storyboards on a film set. *(Sony Pictures Enterprises/ZUMA/Corbis)*

longer was the visually funny slapstick humor enough to make viewers laugh. Much of the humor in sound comedies arose from the script and from the successful direction of professionals like Frank Capra and Ernst Lubitsch.

The U.S. film industry experienced crises and controversy during the next 50 years, including financial problems, conglomerations of studios, and the introduction of the ratings system. New genres and elements began to challenge directorial genius over the years: science fiction, adventure, film noir; graphic representation of violence and sex; and sensational and computer-enhanced special effects. By the 1970s, university film schools had been established and were sending out creative directors, such as Francis Ford Coppola, George Lucas, Martin Scorsese, and Steven Spielberg, to name a few.

The continued development of new technologies has had a remarkable effect on the film and television industries. Advances such as computer-generated animation, digital filming, digital sound, and high-definition television have given directors more tools to work with and the ability to produce an increasing variety of looks, sounds, characters—worlds—in their finished films or shows. Additionally, directors are using technologies not only to shape what the audience sees but also to determine where the audience sees it. Computers and the Internet have a growing role in the motion picture industry, as evidenced by the 2001 launching of the Sundance Online Film Festival, dedicated to highlighting new works designed specifically for presentation on the Web. Such new tools for creating films and TV shows and new avenues for presentation promise continued growth in this creative field.

THE JOB

Film directors, also called *filmmakers,* are considered to bear ultimate responsibility for the tone and quality of the films they work on. They interpret the stories and narratives presented in scripts and coordinate the filming of their interpretations. They are involved in pre-production, production, and postproduction. They audition, select, and rehearse the acting crew; they work on matters regarding set designs, musical scores, and costumes; and they decide on details such as where scenes should be shot, what backgrounds might be needed, and how special effects could be employed.

The director of a film often works with a *casting director,* who is in charge of auditioning performers. The casting director pays close attention to attributes of the performers such as physical appearance, quality of voice, and acting ability and experience, and then presents to the director a list of suitable candidates for each role.

One of the most important aspects of the film director's job is working with the performers. Directors have their own styles of extracting accurate emotion and performance from cast members, but they must be dedicated to this goal.

Two common techniques that categorize directors' styles are montage and mise-en-scene. *Montage directors* are concerned primarily with using editing techniques to produce desired results; they consider it important to focus on how individual shots will work when pieced together with others. Consider Alfred Hitchcock, who directed the production of one scene in *Psycho* by filming discrete shots in a bathroom and then editing in dialogue, sound effects, and music to create tremendous suspense. *Mise-en-scene directors* are more concerned with the pre-editing phase, focusing on the elements of angles, movement, and design one shot at a time, as Orson Welles did. Many directors combine elements of both techniques in their work.

The film's *art director* creates set design concepts and chooses shoot locations. He or she meets with the filmmaker and producer to set budgets and schedules and then accordingly coordinates the construction of sets. Research is done on the period in which the film is to take place, and experts are consulted to help create appropriate architectural and environmental styles. The art director also is often involved in design ideas for costumes, makeup and hairstyles, photographic effects, and other elements of the film's production.

The *director of photography,* or *cinematographer,* is responsible for organizing and implementing the actual camera work. Together with the filmmaker, he or she interprets scenes and decides on appropriate camera motion to achieve desired results. The director of photography determines the amounts of natural and artificial lighting required for each shoot and such technical factors as the type of film to be used, camera angles and distance, depth of field, and focus.

Motion pictures are usually filmed out of sequence, meaning that the ending might be shot first and scenes from the middle of the story might not be filmed until the end of production. Directors are responsible for scheduling each day's sequence of scenes; they coordinate filming so that scenes using the same set and performers will be filmed together. In addition to conferring with the art director and the director of photography, filmmakers meet with technicians and crew members to advise on and approve final scenery, lighting, props, and other necessary equipment. They are also involved with final approval of costumes, choreography, and music.

After all the scenes have been shot, postproduction begins. The director works with picture and sound editors to cut apart and piece together the final reels. The *film editor* shares the director's vision about the picture and assembles shots according to that overall idea, synchronizing film with voice and sound tracks produced by the *sound editor* and *music editor.*

While the director supervises all major aspects of film production, various assistants help throughout the process. In a less creative position than the filmmaker's, the *first assistant director* organizes various practical matters involved during the shooting of each scene. The *second assistant director* is a coordinator who works as a liaison among the production office, the first assistant director, and the performers. The *second unit director* coordinates sequences such as scenic inserts and action shots that do not involve the main acting crew.

REQUIREMENTS

High School
Film directors' careers are nontraditional. There is no standard training outline involved, no normal progression up a movie industry ladder leading to the director's job. At the very least, a high school diploma, while not technically required if you wish to become a director, will still probably be indispensable to you in terms of the

Facts about the Academy Awards and Film Directors

- The first Academy Awards were held on May 16, 1929.
- The Academy Awards, often known as Oscars, are made of gold-plated britannium, a metal alloy. Each award is 13 inches tall and weighs 8 pounds.
- John Ford, director of classic movies such as *Stagecoach, The Quiet Man*, and *Mister Roberts*, won four Oscars for directing—the most of any director in the history of the Academy Awards. William Wyler (*Roman Holiday, Ben Hur, Mrs. Miniver*, and *The Best Years of Our Lives*) places second with three best director Oscars.
- The oldest person awarded an Academy Award in direction was Clint Eastwood for *Million Dollar Baby* (2004). His age: 74 years, 272 days. The youngest? Norman Taurog (32 years, 260 days) for *Skippy* (1930/31).

Source: Academy of Motion Picture Arts and Sciences

background and education it signifies. As is true of all artists, especially those in a medium as widely disseminated as film, you will need to have rich and varied experience in order to create works that are intelligently crafted and speak to people of many different backgrounds. In high school, courses in English, art, theater, and history will give you a good foundation. Further, a high school diploma will be necessary if you decide to go on to film school. Be active in school and community drama productions, whether as performer, set designer, or cue-card holder.

Postsecondary Training

In college and afterward, take film classes and volunteer to work on other students' films. Dedication, talent, and experience have always been indispensable to a director. No doubt it is beneficial to become aware of one's passion for film as early as possible. Woody Allen, for example, recognized early in his life the importance motion pictures held for him, but he worked as a magician, jazz clarinet player, joke writer, and stand-up comic before ever directing films. Allen took few film courses in his life.

On the other hand, many successful directors such as Francis Ford Coppola and Martha Coolidge have taken the formal film school route. There are more than 500 film studies programs offered by schools of higher education throughout the United States, including those considered to be the five most reputable: those of the American Film Institute in Los Angeles, Columbia University in New York City, New York University, the University of California at Los Angeles (UCLA), and the University of Southern California. These schools have film professionals on their faculties and provide a very visible stage for student talent, being located in the two film-business hot spots, California and New York. (The tuition for film programs offered elsewhere, however, tends to be much less expensive than at these schools.)

Film school offers overall formal training, providing an education in fundamental directing skills by working with student productions. Such education is rigorous, but in addition to teaching skills it provides aspiring directors with peer groups and a network of contacts with students, faculty, and guest speakers that can be of help after graduation.

The debate continues on what is more influential in a directing career: film school or personal experience. Some say that it is possible for creative people to land directing jobs without having gone through a formal program. Competition is so pervasive in the industry that even film school graduates find jobs scarce (only 5 to 10 percent of the students who graduate from film schools each year find jobs in the industry). Martha Coolidge, for instance, made independent films for 10 years before directing a Hollywood movie.

Other Requirements

Konstantin Stanislavsky had a passion for his directorial work in the theater, believing that it was an art of immense social importance. Today's motion picture directors must have similar inspiration and possibly even greater creative strength, because of the many more responsibilities involved in directing modern film.

EXPLORING

If you are a would-be director, the most obvious opportunity for exploration lies in your own imagination. Being drawn to films and captivated by the process of how they are made is the beginning of the filmmaker's journey.

In high school and beyond, carefully study and pay attention to motion pictures. Watch them at every opportunity, both at the theater and at home. Two major trade publications to read are *Variety* (http://www.variety.com) and *Hollywood Reporter* (http://www. hollywoodreporter.com). The Directors Guild of America's (DGA) official publication *DGA Magazine* contains much information on the industry. If you are unable to find this magazine at a public library or bookstore, visit the DGA website to read sample articles (address at end of this article). Also, the book *How to Make It in Hollywood: All the Right Moves* (Linda Buzzell, 1996, Harper Perennial) is a very good informal guide that presents insider tips on such factors as "schmoozing" and chutzpah (self-confidence) as well as an extensive list of valuable resources. Young women interested in learning more about becoming film directors should obtain a copy of *Girl Director: A How-To Guide for the First-Time, Flat-Broke, Film and Video Maker* (Berkeley, Calif: Ten Speed Press, 2005). This useful book offers a lengthy history of women directors and features expert advice on choosing a camera, setting up and framing shots, editing, and creating animated films.

During summers, many camps and workshops offer programs for high school students interested in film work. For example, UCLA presents its Media Workshops for students aged 14 to 24. Classes there focus on mass media production, including film, TV, and video. For information, contact the Media Workshops Foundation, Tel: 800-223-4561, http://www.reddelicious.com/mediaworkshops/foundation.

EMPLOYERS

Employment as a film director is usually on a freelance or contractual basis. Directors find work, for example, with film studios (both major and independent), at television stations and cable networks, through advertising agencies, with record companies, and through the creation of their own independent film projects.

STARTING OUT

It is considered difficult to begin as a motion picture director. With nontraditional steps to professional status, the occupation poses challenges for those seeking employment. However, there is somewhat solid advice for those who wish to direct motion pictures.

Many current directors began their careers in other film industry professions, such as acting or writing. Consider Jodie Foster, who appeared in 30 films and dozens of television productions before she went on to direct her first motion picture at the age of 28. Obviously it helps to grow up near the heart of "Tinseltown" and to have the influence of one's family spurring you on. The support of family and friends is often cited as an essential element in shaping the confidence you need to succeed in the industry.

As mentioned earlier, film school is a breeding ground for making contacts in the industry. Often, contacts are the essential factor in getting a job; many Hollywood insiders agree that it's not what you know but who you know that will get you in. Networking often leads to good opportunities at various types of jobs in the industry. Many professionals recommend that those who want to become directors should go to Los Angeles or New York, find any industry-related job, continue to take classes, and keep their eyes and ears open for news of job openings, especially with those professionals who are admired for their talent.

A program to be aware of is the Assistant Directors Training Program of the Directors Guild of America (address is listed at the end of this article). This program provides an excellent opportunity to those without industry connections to work on film and television productions. The program is based at two locations, New York City for the East Coast program and Sherman Oaks, California, for the West Coast program. Trainees receive hands-on experience, through placement with major studios or on television movies and series, and education, through mandatory seminars. The East Coast program requires trainees to complete up to 350 days of on-set production work; the West Coast program requires 400 days. While they are working, trainees are paid, beginning with a weekly salary of $540 in the East and $578 in the West. Once trainees have completed their program, they become freelance second assistant directors and can join the guild. The competition is extremely stiff for these positions; each location usually accepts 20 or fewer trainees from among some 800 to 1,200 applicants each year.

Keep in mind that major studios in Hollywood is not the only place where directors work. Directors also work on documentaries, on television productions, and with various types of video presentations, from music to business. Honing skills at these types of jobs is beneficial for those still intent on directing the big screen.

ADVANCEMENT

In the motion picture industry, advancement often comes with recognition. Directors who work on well-received movies are given awards as well as further job offers. Probably the most glamorized trophy is the Academy Award: the Oscar. Oscars are awarded in 24 categories, including one for best achievement in directing, and are given annually at a gala to recognize the outstanding accomplishments of those in the field.

Candidates for Oscars are usually judged by peers. Directors who have not worked on films popular enough to have made it in

Hollywood should nevertheless seek recognition from reputable organizations. One such group is the National Endowment for the Arts, an independent agency of the U.S. government that supports and awards artists, including those who work in film. The endowment provides financial assistance in the form of fellowships and grants to those seen as contributing to the excellence of arts in the country.

EARNINGS

Directors' salaries vary greatly. Most Hollywood film directors are members of the Directors Guild of America, and salaries (as well as hours of work and other employment conditions) are usually negotiated by this union. Generally, contracts provide for minimum weekly salaries and follow a basic trend depending on the cost of the picture being produced: for film budgets over $1.5 million, the weekly salary is about $13,420; for budgets of $500,000 to $1.5 million, it is approximately $9,580 per week; and for budgets under $500,000, the weekly salary is approximately $8,400. Keep in mind that because directors are freelancers, they may have no income for many weeks out of the year.

Although contracts usually provide only for the minimum rate of pay, most directors earn more, and they often negotiate extra conditions. Woody Allen, for example, takes the minimum salary required by the union for directing a film but also receives at least 10 percent of the film's gross receipts.

The U.S. Department of Labor reports that film directors and producers had mean annual earnings of $99,160 in 2004. The lowest 10 percent of directors and producers employed in all industries (including film) earned less than $26,320. Top directors can earn millions of dollars per film.

WORK ENVIRONMENT

The work of the director is considered glamorous and prestigious, and of course directors have been known to become quite famous. But directors work under great stress, meeting deadlines, staying within budgets, and resolving problems among staff. "Nine-to-five" definitely does not describe a day in the life of a director; 16-hour days (and more) are not uncommon. Because directors are ultimately responsible for so much, schedules often dictate that they become immersed in their work around the clock, from preproduction to final cut. Nonetheless, those able to make it in the industry find their work to be extremely enjoyable and satisfying.

OUTLOOK

According to the U.S. Department of Labor, employment for motion picture and television directors is expected to grow about as fast as the average for all occupations through 2012. This forecast is based on the increasing global demand for films and television programming made in the United States as well as continuing U.S. demand for home video and DVD rentals. However, competition is extreme and turnover is high. Most positions in the motion picture industry are held on a freelance basis. As is the case with most film industry workers, directors are usually hired to work on one film at a time. After a film is completed, new contacts must be made for further assignments.

FOR MORE INFORMATION

For information on the AFI Conservatory, AFI workshops, AFI awards, and other film and television news, visit the AFI website or contact
American Film Institute (AFI)
2021 North Western Avenue
Los Angeles, CA 90027-1657
Tel: 323-856-7600
http://www.afi.com

Visit the DGA website to read selections from the DGA Magazine, get industry news, and find links to film schools and film festivals.
Directors Guild of America (DGA)
7920 Sunset Boulevard
Los Angeles, CA 90046
Tel: 310-289-2000
http://www.dga.org

For more information about DGA's Assistant Directors Training Program, visit the following websites:
East Coast Program
http://www.dgatrainingprogram.org

West Coast Program
http://www.trainingplan.org

Film Editors

QUICK FACTS

School Subjects
Art
English

Personal Skills
Artistic
Communication/ideas

Work Environment
Primarily indoors
Primarily one location

Minimum Education Level
High school diploma

Salary Range
$21,710 to $43,590 to
$93,950+

Certification or Licensing
None available

Outlook
Faster than the average

DOT
962

GOE
01.08.01

NOC
5131

O*NET-SOC
27-4032.00

OVERVIEW

Film editors perform an essential role in the motion picture and television industries. They take an unedited draft of film or videotape and use specialized equipment to improve the draft until it is ready for viewing. It is the responsibility of the film editor to create the most effective film possible. There are approximately 15,180 film and television editors employed in the United States.

HISTORY

Early film editing was sometimes done by directors, studio technicians, or others for whom this was not their specialty. Now every film, including the most brief television advertisement, has a film editor who is responsible for the continuity and clarity of the film.

The motion picture and television industries have experienced substantial growth in the last few years in the United States. The effects of this growth has resulted in a steady demand for the essential skills that film editors provide. With recent innovations in computer technology, much of the work performed by film editors uses sophisticated computer programs. All of these factors have enabled many film editors to find steady work as salaried employees of film and television production companies and as independent contractors who provide their services on a per-job basis.

THE JOB

Film editors work closely with producers and directors throughout an entire project. These editors assist in the earliest phase, called pre-

92

production, and during the production phase, when actual filming occurs. Their skills are in the greatest demand during postproduction, the completion of primary filming. During preproduction, editors meet with producers to learn about the objectives of the film or video. If the project is a feature-length motion picture, the editor must understand the story line. The producer may explain the larger scope of the project so that the editor knows the best way to approach the work when it is time to edit the film. In consultation with the director, editors may discuss the best way to present the screenplay or script. They may discuss different settings, scenes, or camera angles even before filming or taping begins. With this kind of preparation, film editors are ready to practice their craft as soon as the production phase is complete.

Feature-length films, of course, take much more time to edit than television commercials. Therefore, some editors may spend months on one project, while others may be working on several shorter projects simultaneously.

Steve Swersky owns his own editorial company in Santa Monica, California, and he has done editing for commercials, films, and TV. In addition to editing many Jeep commercials and coming-attractions trailers for such movies as *Titanic, Fargo,* and *The Usual Suspects,* Swersky has worked on 12 films. Though commercials can be edited quickly, a film project can possibly take six to nine months to edit.

Swersky's work involves taking the film that has been developed in labs and transferring it to videotape for him to watch. He uses "nonlinear" computer editing for his projects, as opposed to traditional "linear" systems involving many video players and screens. "The difference between linear and nonlinear editing," he says, "is like the difference between typing and using a word processor. When you want to change a written page, you have to retype it; with word processing you can just cut and paste."

Swersky uses the Lightworks nonlinear editing system. With this system, he converts the film footage to a digital format. The computer has a database that tracks individual frames and puts all the scenes together in a folder of information. This information is stored on a hard drive and can instantly be brought up on a screen, allowing an editor to access scenes and frames with the click of a mouse.

Film editors are usually the final decision makers when it comes to choosing which segments will stay in as they are, which segments will be cut, or which may need to be redone. Editors look at the quality of the segment, its dramatic value, and its relationship to other segments. They then arrange the segments in an order that creates the most effective finished product. "I assemble the scenes," Swersky

A film student learns the art of film editing. *(Jeff Greenberg, Index Stock Imagery)*

says, "choosing what is the best, what conveys the most emotion. I bring the film to life, in a way."

He relies on the script and notes from the director, along with his natural sense of how a scene should progress, in putting together the film, commercial, or show. He looks for the best shots, camera angles, line deliveries, and continuity.

Some editors specialize in certain areas of film. *Sound editors* work on the soundtracks of television programs or motion pictures. They often keep libraries of sounds that they reuse for various projects. These include natural sounds, such as thunder or raindrops, animal noises, motor sounds, or musical interludes. Some sound editors specialize in music and may have training in music theory or performance. Others work with sound effects. They may use unusual objects, machines, or computer-generated noisemakers to create a desired sound for a film.

REQUIREMENTS

High School

Broadcast journalism and other media and communications courses will provide you with some practical experience in video editing. Because film editing requires creativity along with technical skills, you should take English, speech, theater, and other courses that will allow you to develop writing skills. Art and photography classes will involve you with visual media. Because of the technical nature of film editing, take computer classes to become comfortable and confident using basic computer programs.

Postsecondary Training

Some studios require a bachelor's degree for those seeking positions as film editors. Yet actual on-the-job experience is the best guarantee of securing lasting employment. Degrees in liberal arts fields are preferred, but courses in cinematography and audiovisual techniques help film editors get started in their work. You may choose to pursue a degree in such subjects as English, journalism, theater, or film. Community and two-year colleges often offer courses in the study of film as literature. Some of these colleges also teach film editing. Universities with departments of broadcast journalism offer courses in film editing and also may have contacts at local television stations. The American Film Institute hosts an educational website (http://www.afi.edu) that offers listings of high schools with film courses and other resources for teachers and students.

Training as a film or television editor takes from four to 10 years. Many editors learn much of their work on the job as an assistant or apprentice at larger studios that offer these positions. During an apprenticeship, the apprentice has the opportunity to see the work of the editor up close. The editor may eventually assign some of his or her minor duties to the apprentice, while the editor makes the larger decisions. After a few years the apprentice may be promoted to editor or may apply for a position as a film editor at other studios. Training in film editing is also available in the military, including the Air Force, Marine Corps, Coast Guard, and Navy.

Other Requirements

You should be able to work cooperatively with other creative people when editing a film. You should remain open to suggestions and guidance, while also maintaining your confidence in the presence of other professionals. A successful editor has an understanding of the history of film and television and a feel for the narrative form in general. Computer skills are also important and will help you to learn new technology in the field. You may be required to join a union to do this work, depending on the studio.

"You should have a good visual understanding," Steve Swersky says. "You need to be able to tell a story, and be aware of everything that's going on in a frame."

EXPLORING

Many high schools have film clubs, and some have cable television stations affiliated with the school district. Often school-run television channels give students the opportunity to create and edit short programs. Check out what's available at your school.

One of the best way to prepare for a career as a film editor is to read widely. By reading literature, you will get a sense of the different ways in which stories can be presented. Some high schools even offer film classes.

You should be familiar with many different kinds of films, including documentaries, short films, and feature films. Don't just watch the films you rent from the video store; rather, study them, paying close attention to the decisions the editors made in piecing together the scenes. You might also want to check out *The Cutting Edge: The Magic of Movie Editing* (Warner Home Video, 2005) for an inside look at the world of film editing.

Large television stations and film companies occasionally have volunteers or student interns. Most people in the film industry start out doing minor tasks helping with production. These production assistants get the opportunity to see all of the film professionals at work. By working closely with a film editor, a production assistant can learn television or film operations as well as specific film editing techniques.

EMPLOYERS

Approximately 15,180 film and television editors are employed in the United States. Some film editors work primarily with news programs, documentaries, or special features. They may develop ongoing working relationships with directors or producers who hire them from one project to another. Many film editors who have worked for a studio or postproduction company for several years often become independent contractors. They offer their services on a per-job basis to producers of films and advertisements, negotiating their own fees, and typically have purchased or leased their own editing equipment.

STARTING OUT

With a minimum of a high school diploma or a degree from a two-year college, you can apply for entry-level jobs in many film or television studios. Most studios, however, will not consider people for film editor positions without a bachelor's degree or several years of on-the-job experience. Larger studios may offer apprenticeships for film editors. Apprentices has the opportunity to see the work of the film editor up close. The film editor may eventually assign some of his or her minor duties to the apprentice, while the film editor makes the larger decisions. After a few years, the apprentice may be promoted to film editor or may apply for a position as a film editor at other studios.

Those who have completed bachelor's or master's degrees have typically gained hands-on experience through school projects. Another benefit of going to school is that contacts that you make while in school, both through your school's career services office and alumni, can be a valuable resource when you look for your first job. Your school's career services office may also have listings of job openings. Some studio work is union regulated. Therefore you may also want to contact union locals to find out about job requirements and openings.

ADVANCEMENT

Once film editors have secured employment in their field, their advancement comes with further experience and greater recognition. Some film editors develop good working relationships with directors or producers. These film editors may be willing to leave the security of a studio job for the possibility of working one-on-one with the director or producer on a project. These opportunities often provide film editors with the autonomy they may not get in their regular jobs. Some are willing to take a pay cut to work on a project they feel is important.

Some film editors choose to stay at their studios and advance through seniority to editing positions with higher salaries. They may be able to negotiate better benefits packages or to choose the films they will work on. They may also choose which directors they wish to work with. In larger studios, they may train and supervise staffs of less experienced or apprentice film editors.

"I want to continue doing films," Steve Swersky says. "Every film is a step up the ladder on the long way to the top." He plans to continue to work on commercials, but would also like to work on films with bigger budgets and more prestige. "I'd like to be at the Academy Awards someday," he says, "accepting the Oscar for film editing."

EARNINGS

Film editors are not as highly paid as others working in their industry. They have less clout than directors or producers, but they have more authority in the production of a project than many other film technicians. According to the U.S. Department of Labor, the median annual wage for film and video editors was $43,590 in 2004. The lowest paid 10 percent of film and video editors earned less than $21,710 a year, while the highest paid 10 percent earned over $93,950. The most experienced and sought-after film editors can command much higher salaries.

WORK ENVIRONMENT

Most of the work done by film editors is done in film studios or at postproduction companies using editing equipment. The working environment is often a small, cramped studio office. Working hours vary widely depending on the film. During the filming of a commercial, for instance, film editors may be required to work overtime, at night, or on weekends to finish the project by an assigned date. Many feature-length films are kept on tight production schedules that allow for steady work unless filming gets behind.

"As stressful as the work can be," Steve Swersky says, "we joke around that it's not like having a real job. Every day is a fun day."

During filming, film editors may be asked to be on hand at the filming location. Locations may be outdoors or in other cities, and travel is occasionally required. More often, however, the film editor edits in the studio, where the bulk of his or her time is spent.

Disadvantages of the job involve the editor's low rank on the totem pole of film or television industry jobs. However, most film editors feel that this is outweighed by the advantages. Film editors can view the films on which they have worked and be proud of their role in creating them.

OUTLOOK

The outlook for film and television editors is very good. In fact, the U.S. Department of Labor predicts faster-than-average employment growth for film and television editors through 2012. The growth of cable television and an increase in the number of independent film studios will translate into greater demand for editors. This will also force the largest studios to offer more competitive salaries in order to attract the best film and television editors.

The digital revolution has greatly affected film editing. Editors now work much more closely with special effects houses in putting together films. When using more effects, film editors have to edit scenes with an eye towards special effects to be added later. Digital editing systems are also available for home computers—users can feed their own digital video into their computers, then edit the material, and add their own special effects and titles. This technology may allow some prospective film editors more direct routes into the industry, but the majority of editors will have to follow traditional routes, obtaining years of hands-on experience.

FOR MORE INFORMATION

The ACE features some career information on its website, along with information about internship opportunities and sample articles from CinemaEditor Magazine.
   American Cinema Editors
   100 Universal City Plaza
   Building 2352, Room 202
   Universal City, CA 91608
   Tel: 818-777-2900
   http://www.ace-filmeditors.org

For information about schools with film and television programs of study and to read interviews with filmmakers, visit the AFI website.
   American Film Institute
   2021 North Western Avenue
   Los Angeles, CA 90027-1657
   Tel: 323-856-7600
   http://www.afi.com

=== **INTERVIEW** ===

Kevin Tent has worked as a film editor on many popular and critically acclaimed films, including Election, About Schmidt, *and* Sideways. *He was kind enough to discuss his interesting career with the editors of* Careers in Focus: Film

   Q.   What made you decide to become a film editor?
   A.   I never intended to be a film editor. I knew that I wanted to do something in film or television from when I was about 16 or 17. I didn't know what. When the time for college came around (without any real direction or vision), I opted for a school that specialized in communications and broadcasting degrees.

   After about two years I realized that television news and broadcasting in general was not what I was interested in. I guess I was looking for something more artistic. There was a sort of conscious/subconscious feeling that perhaps working in movies was what I was looking for. So I dropped out of school and moved to California. (That's where they make movies, right?) After being there for a short time I heard of a school called Los Angeles City College. It was the perfect place for me—"a school of hard knocks" as the saying goes. They basically gave you a camera and told you to come back in two weeks with a short film.

While working on one of my short films I remember very clearly a moment when I was shocked by the power of editing. For what seemed like weeks I was working and laboring trying to get my film to play better. A friend of mine stopped by the cutting room and said, "Why don't you just cut that part out and go to that?" I tried what he had said, and it was soooo much better. It was an epiphany. From that point on I had a new respect and small realization of the power of editing.

After two years it was time for me to leave Los Angeles City College. With my two short "final" film projects in hand I got an interview with a small educational film company that was looking for a staff editor. Mind you these films were nothing spectacular. They were your basic educational films. Static, boring, and unoriginal. But it was a job and I was glad to have it. I learned a lot and pretty much did everything relating to the post-production of a film. I didn't cut the negative, but I cut the sound effects, sometimes the music. I would supervise the mix and get the films pushed through the lab. Much of this work was not always creative, but definitely good to know. My education was continuing. At this time I still didn't consider myself an editor, "These are just ridiculous educational films," I thought. "I'm not a real editor." But a producer/friend of mine set me straight. "What do they pay you to do?" he asked. "Edit," I replied. "Then you're an editor you dope!"

That was the first time I ever thought of myself as an editor. It was also the first time I really started to get into it. In my free time I would help friends edit their short films, and I started to become more conscious of the profession as a whole.

After a couple of years at the educational film company I heard about a job at a low-budget film company. They had a problematic film, and they wanted somebody to recut it. They also wanted somebody to just take the whole thing and finish it— supervise the mix and get it pushed through the lab (all the things I had been doing at the educational film company). A door opened and I was ready to walk through it. From that re-cut I got my first job editing a feature film. From that point on I began to consider myself an editor. It was never a conscious decision to become one. It just happened. Thank goodness.

Q. What are the characteristics of a well-edited film?

A. Well, that's a difficult question. All films are different and I suppose a well-edited film is one where the style of editing fits the tone and style of the film in general. It's also been said, and I think it's true, that editing should be pretty much invisible—meaning that an audience should not notice the editing at a conscious level but just feel at a sub-conscious/emotional level.

For instance, a horror movie will usually build in creepiness to a scare. Issues to consider include how long to hold on the look of a character, how long to hold on what the audience is seeing, and how long to let a scene build before its climax. Then if there is a scare, do you decide to cut more quickly? Does sudden rapid cutting heighten the anxiety for the audience? These are all things the editor and director must consider while editing.

This is just an example of cutting a few scenes. Editors, along with the director, have to feel how these scenes play in the movie as a whole. Overall pace is an important issue that the editor has to keep in mind. All of us have seen movies where it seems like nothing is happening. If an audience gets bored and you lose their patience, then you're in trouble.

Q. What is your most memorable film project as an editor and why?

A. So many of the films I've worked on are memorable. I've learned and am proud of just about every movie I've cut. I'd have to say though that *Election* is one of my favorites—so far that is. I'm not done yet. I had worked with Alexander Payne on his first film, *Citizen Ruth,* and, fortunately, he asked me to cut his next endeavor, *Election.* Even in the script stage the story was filled with many "filmic" devices. There was voice-over, freeze frames, multiple characters, multiple points of view, parallel stories, and everything tying up in the end. An editor's dream! It had big ambitions, but at the same time was a small independent film.

In any position in the film business one hopes they get an opportunity to work on a film like *Election:* an original screenplay with a talented cast and director. A film, when finished, that breaks out from the pack, and is loved by both critics and audiences alike. The thing is, we didn't know at the time it would be as successful as it was. I always knew the film was special. And I always loved it, but I didn't expect it to be the sort of underground hit it became.

Especially since we had something like seven studio screenings (with test audiences) and it never did well at any of them. In fact, the film generally tested poorly with the recruited audiences. As it was we worked very long and hard on the picture, which is I think one of the reasons for its success.

As an editor I learned a lot working on *Election*. I learned to be more open to new and unusual ideas. Alexander Payne is an excellent director on many levels. He tries to keep the cutting room free so creative thoughts can be expressed without judgment or I should say pre-judgment. Working with him on *Election* was an all-around great experience. Sure we had dark times of fear and depression, but for the most part we had a blast cutting the film. And then for it to be received as well as it was just icing on the cake. The exact same thing happened with Alexander's *About Schmidt* and especially *Sideways*.

Q. What do you like most about your job?

A. I'd have to say that the best part of the job is working with the directors. They are usually amazing, extremely interesting people. I often wonder what drives them, where do they get their ideas. They often put everything on the line to make their film. As the editor you become their partner and their closest confidant—and often their protector. Protecting them from studios, producers, and sometimes themselves. I like to think that when the editing room door closes what goes on inside is kind of magic. Sometimes the director has a vision of his or her film overall, but sometimes the vision isn't clear yet. They have a general idea of what they're looking for but it's not exact—much like the idea I had for working in the film industry. It was a hunch or an instinct more than a clearcut idea. Same goes for directors and their films. The fun is working on the film and making the vision come into focus. It's so exciting to bounce around ideas and slowly, but surely, make the film better. When the door opens and we walk out at the end of the day, hopefully the film is a little bit better.

Also, as the editor, you're one of the few people besides the director and maybe producer who has the opportunity to have such a long relationship with the film. Nobody but usually the director knows the film better than you. It's a wonderful experience to see it evolve. It's very exciting.

Q. What advice would you give to high school students who are interested in this career?

A. I get asked this question a lot. There are no right or wrong paths to a career in editing. Like everything you keep on moving forward. I think watching films and talking about them is a great thing to do. But so is looking at paintings, studying art, listening to music, or reading books. When you're young (and even when you're older) I think the most important thing to do is absorb. Always be like a sponge. I like to think of editing as an art form. So I think editors should think like artists. When I was in high school I did the follow spot for school plays. I didn't do it because I thought it would help me in a film career. I just did it because it was fun. Just keep doing stuff and trying different things. Absorb. All that experimentation is good for you especially at a young age. Think like an artist.

I also think taking basic psychology or communication classes could be good. Understanding people is important in any profession and the film industry is no different. Editors should be good listeners and communicators.

Most important, though, I think people who really want to cut should just edit. Use iMovie or whatever and just cut stuff. Edit your little brother's birthday party or sister's wedding video. Or make a short film or a music video with your friends. Be an editor. You will learn by doing and also learn if it's really something that suits you. And don't be afraid to experiment. Do a version of your sister's wedding with crazy funky music or intercut it with stills from when she was little. Have fun with it. She may not like it, but just cut one version for her and one or two versions for you. Just cut as many things as possible and experiment while doing it.

Q. What are the three most important professional qualities for film editors?

A. Probably number one is getting along with people. The film industry is a very people-oriented business. Having some understanding of how people click is really helpful. Just because you're in a dark little editing room all day doesn't mean you're not dealing with a lot of humans and their emotions.

As stated earlier I think being a good listener and a good communicator is also really important. Being able to understand what a director is saying even if he or she can't articulate exactly what they mean. Many times you have to read between the lines. Understanding people is a great advantage.

I also guess having a good work ethic is important. Again, like many professions film editing is a very competitive field. There are many people trying to do what you do. Talent alone won't do the trick. I worked very hard on very low budget pictures for years. I just kept working and learning one step at a time. A career in any profession takes time and energy. It's not a sprint. It's a marathon. Willingness to work hard is a great attribute to have.

Film Writers

OVERVIEW

Film writers express, edit, promote, and interpret ideas and facts about films and the motion picture industry in written form for newspapers, magazines, books, websites, and radio and television broadcasts. There are approximately 139,000 salaried writers in the United States; only a small percentage of this number are film writers.

HISTORY

The famous inventor Thomas Edison produced a short movie called *The Sneeze* in 1894, using film for the first time instead of individual plates. Georges Melies introduced narrative films in 1899 in France, and in 1903 Edwin Porter filmed *The Great Train Robbery,* the first motion picture that told a story using modern filming techniques.

Motion pictures became increasingly popular in the early 1900s, with the advent of the movie house and silent film stars such as Charlie Chaplin and Rudolph Valentino. It was not until 1927, when *The Jazz Singer* with Al Jolson was produced, that talking movies began to be made.

As the film industry grew, so did the number of publications that began to cover this fast-growing and glamorous industry. Some, such as *Variety* (founded in 1905) and *Hollywood Reporter* (1930), are still reporting on the film industry today.

In addition to the print media, the broadcasting industry has contributed to the development of the professional film writer. Radio, television, and the Internet are sources of information, education, and entertainment that provide employment for thousands of film writers.

QUICK FACTS

School Subjects
English
Journalism

Personal Skills
Communication/ideas
Helping/teaching

Work Environment
Primarily indoors
One location with some
travel

Minimum Education Level
Bachelor's degree

Salary Range
$23,330 to $45,490 to
$91,260+

Certification or Licensing
None available

Outlook
About as fast as the average

DOT
131

GOE
01.02.01

NOC
5121

O*NET-SOC
27-3043.00

THE JOB

Film writers write about the motion picture industry, its actors and other professionals, films, genres, companies, events, history, and any other topic that relates to the field. The nature of their work is as varied as the venues for which they write: newspapers, magazines, books, and websites and blogs. Some film writers also appear on television and radio talk shows and documentaries.

Film staff writers are employed by magazines and newspapers to write news stories, feature articles, and columns about the film industry. First they come up with an idea for an article from their own interests or are assigned a topic by an editor. The topic is of relevance to the particular publication; for example, a writer for an animation magazine may be assigned an article on the Academy Award for animation. A writer for a film history magazine may come up with the idea of interviewing one of the last remaining lead actors from a famous film such as *Casablanca*. A writer for a weekly entertainment section in a newspaper may be assigned to interview the lead actor in the latest science fiction blockbuster.

After writers receive their assignments, they begin gathering as much information as possible about the subject through library research, interviews, the Internet, observation, and other methods. They keep extensive notes from which they will draw material for their project. Once the material has been organized and arranged in logical sequence, writers prepare a written outline. The process of developing a piece of writing is exciting, although it can also involve detailed and solitary work. After researching an idea, a writer might discover that a different perspective or related topic would be more effective, entertaining, or marketable.

When working on assignment, writers usually submit their outlines to an editor or other company representative for approval. Then they write a first draft, trying to put the material into words that will have the desired effect on their audience. They often rewrite or polish sections of the material as they proceed, always searching for just the right way of imparting information or expressing an idea or opinion. A manuscript may be reviewed, corrected, and revised numerous times before a final copy is submitted. Even after that, an editor may request additional changes.

Film columnists or *commentators* analyze news and social issues as they relate to the motion picture industry. They write about events from the standpoint of their own experience or opinion.

Film critics review movies for print publications and television and radio stations. They tell readers and listeners why or why not, in

Useful Websites for Film Writers

FilmCritic.com
http://www.filmcritic.com

Film Festivals.com
http://www.filmfestivals.com

Internet Movie Database
http://www.imdb.com

Metacritic.com/Film
http://www.metacritic.com/film

Movie City News
http://www.moviecitynews.com

Reelviews
http://movie-reviews.colossus.net

Roger Ebert.com
http://rogerebert.suntimes.com

Senses of Cinema
http://www.sensesofcinema.com

their opinion, they should spend their money to see a movie. Film critics may also interview actors, directors, and other film professionals for print articles and broadcast interviews. Some film critics, such as Roger Ebert, become celebrities in their own right.

Writers can be employed either as in-house staff or as freelancers. Pay varies according to experience and the position, but freelancers must provide their own office space and equipment such as computers and fax machines. Freelancers also are responsible for keeping tax records, sending out invoices, negotiating contracts, and providing their own health insurance.

REQUIREMENTS

High School
While in high school, build a broad educational foundation by taking courses in English, literature, foreign languages, history, general

science, social studies, computer science, and typing. The ability to type is almost a requisite for many positions in the journalism field, as is familiarity with computers. If you are interested in becoming a film writer, you should watch as many films as possible, as well as read publications on film.

Postsecondary Training

Competition for journalistic writing jobs almost always demands the background of a college education. Many employers prefer you have a broad liberal arts background or majors in English, literature, history, philosophy, or one of the social sciences. Other employers desire communications or journalism training in college. Occasionally a master's degree in a specialized writing field may be required. A number of schools offer courses in journalism, and some of them offer courses or majors in newspaper and magazine writing, publication management, book publishing, and writing for the Internet. If you are interested in film writing, you might want to consider a major, or at least a minor, in a film-related area.

In addition to formal course work, most employers look for practical writing experience. If you have worked on high school or college newspapers, yearbooks, or literary magazines, you will make a better candidate, as well as if you have worked for small community newspapers or radio stations, even in an unpaid position. Many magazines, newspapers, and radio and television stations have summer internship programs that provide valuable training if you want to learn about the publishing and broadcasting businesses. Interns do many simple tasks, such as running errands and answering phones, but some may be asked to perform research, conduct interviews, or even write some minor pieces.

Other Requirements

To be a film writer, you should be creative and able to express ideas clearly, have a broad general knowledge, be skilled in research techniques, have a love of films and film history, and be computer literate. Other assets include curiosity, persistence, initiative, resourcefulness, and an accurate memory. For some jobs—on a newspaper, for example, where the activity is hectic and deadlines are short—the ability to concentrate and produce under pressure is essential. Film critics and columnists need to be confident about their opinions and able to accept criticism from others who may not agree with their views on a film or a film-related topic.

EXPLORING

Jobs in bookstores, magazine shops, and even newsstands will offer you a chance to become familiar with various publications. Major film publications to read include *Variety* (http://www.variety.com), *Hollywood Reporter* (http://www.hollywoodreporter.com), *Premiere* (http://www.premiere.com), *Entertainment Weekly* (http://www.ew.com), Cinefex *(http://www.cinefex.com), The Hollywood Scriptwriter* (http://www.hollywoodscriptwriter.com), *Animation Journal* (http://www.animationjournal.com), and *Animation World* (http://mag.awn.com).

As a high school or college student, you can test your interest and aptitude in the field of writing by serving as a reporter or writer on school newspapers, yearbooks, and literary magazines. Perhaps you could write movie reviews for your school newspaper or an article about a particular film genre or movement for your school's literary magazine. There are also many websites where amateur film critics can post their reviews. Of course, you can always write movie reviews and articles on your own for practice. Small community newspapers often welcome contributions from outside sources, although they may not have the resources to pay for them. Be sure to take as many writing courses and workshops as you can to help you sharpen your writing skills. You might also consider picking up a copy of *A Short Guide to Writing About Film* (New York: Longman, 2003) to help you learn more about writing about film.

You can also obtain information on writing as a career by visiting local newspapers and publishers and interviewing some of the writers who work there. Career conferences and other guidance programs frequently include speakers on the entire field of journalism from local or national organizations.

EMPLOYERS

Only a small percentage of the approximately 139,000 writers and authors in the United States specialize in writing about film. More than one-half of salaried writers and editors work for newspapers, magazines, and book publishers; radio and television broadcasting companies; and Internet publishing and broadcasting companies. Outside the field of journalism, writers are also employed by advertising agencies, public relations firms, and for journals and newsletters published by business and nonprofit organizations, such as professional associations, labor unions, and religious organizations. Other nonjournalism employers are government agencies and film production companies. Other writers work as novelists, short story writers, poets, playwrights, and screenwriters.

The major newspaper, magazine, and book publishers account for the concentration of journalistic writers in large cities such as New York, Chicago, Los Angeles, Boston, Philadelphia, San Francisco, and Washington, D.C. Opportunities with small publishers can be found throughout the country.

STARTING OUT

You will need a good amount of experience to gain a high-level position in the field. Nearly all film writers start out in entry-level positions. These jobs may be listed with college career services offices, or they may be obtained by applying directly to the employment departments of the individual publishers or broadcasting companies. Graduates who previously served internships with these companies often have the advantage of knowing someone who can give them a personal recommendation. Want ads in newspapers and trade journals are another source for jobs. Because of the competition for positions, however, few vacancies are listed with public or private employment agencies.

Employers in the field of journalism usually are interested in samples of published writing. These are often assembled in an organized portfolio or scrapbook. Bylined or signed articles are more credible (and, as a result, more useful) than stories whose source is not identified.

Beginning positions as a junior writer usually involve library research, preparation of rough drafts for part or all of a report, cataloging, and other related writing tasks. These are generally carried on under the supervision of a senior writer.

ADVANCEMENT

Most film writers find their first jobs as editorial, production, or research assistants. Advancement may be more rapid in small media companies, where beginners learn by doing a little bit of everything and may be given writing tasks immediately. At large publishers or broadcast companies, duties are usually more compartmentalized. Assistants in entry-level positions are assigned such tasks as research and fact checking, but it generally takes much longer to advance to full-scale writing duties.

Promotion into higher-level positions may come with the assignment of more important articles and stories to write, or it may be the result of moving to another company. Mobility among employees in this field is common. A staff film writer at a small magazine publisher may switch to a similar position at a more prestigious publication.

Freelance or self-employed writers earn advancement in the form of larger fees as they gain exposure and establish their reputations.

EARNINGS

In 2004, salaried writers had earnings that ranged from less than $23,330 to more than $91,260, according to the U.S. Department of Labor. Writers employed by newspaper and book publishers had annual mean earnings of $45,490. Some film writers also work in radio and television broadcasting. The mean annual salary for writers employed in these industries was $43,260 in 2004.

In addition to their salaries, many film writers earn some income from freelance work. Part-time freelancers may earn from $5,000 to $15,000 a year. Freelance earnings vary widely. Full time established freelance writers may earn $75,000 or more a year.

WORK ENVIRONMENT

Working conditions vary for film writers. Although their workweek usually runs 35 to 40 hours, many writers work overtime. A publication that is issued frequently has more deadlines closer together, creating greater pressures to meet them. The work is especially hectic on newspapers, which operate seven days a week. Writers often work nights and weekends to meet deadlines or to cover a late-developing story.

Most writers work independently, but they often must cooperate with editors, artists, photographers, and rewriters who may have widely differing ideas of how the materials should be prepared and presented.

Physical surroundings range from comfortable private offices to noisy, crowded newsrooms filled with other workers typing and talking on the telephone. Some writers must confine their research to the library or telephone interviews, but others may travel to movie theaters, press conferences, movie sets, award shows, or other offices.

The work is arduous, but most film writers are seldom bored. The most difficult element is the continual pressure of deadlines. People who are the most content as film writers enjoy and work well with deadline pressure.

OUTLOOK

The employment of all writers is expected to increase about as fast as the average rate of all occupations through 2012, according to the U.S. Department of Labor. The demand for writers by newspapers, periodicals, and book publishers is expected to increase. The growth of online publishing on company websites and other online services will also demand many talented writers; those with computer skills will be at an advantage as a result.

People entering the field of writing, especially film writing, should realize that the competition for jobs is extremely keen. Beginners, especially, may have difficulty finding employment. Of the thousands who graduate each year with degrees in English, journalism, communications, and the liberal arts, intending to establish a career as a writer, many turn to other occupations when they find that applicants far outnumber the job openings available.

Potential film writers who end up working in a field other than journalism may be able to earn some income as freelancers, selling articles, stories, books, and possibly TV and movie scripts, but it is usually difficult for anyone to be self-supporting entirely on independent writing.

FOR MORE INFORMATION

For a list of accredited programs in journalism and mass communications, visit the ACEJMC website.
> Accrediting Council on Education in Journalism and Mass
>   Communications (ACEJMC)
> University of Kansas School of Journalism and Mass
>   Communications
> 1435 Jayhawk Boulevard, Stauffer-Flint Hall
> Lawrence, KS 66045-7575
> http://www.ku.edu/~acejmc

This organization provides general educational information on all areas of journalism, including newspapers, magazines, television, and radio.
> Association for Education in Journalism and Mass
>   Communication
> 234 Outlet Pointe Boulevard
> Columbia, SC 29210-5667
> Tel: 803-798-0271
> Email: aejmchq@aejmc.org
> http://www.aejmc.org

The MPA is a good source of information about internships.
Magazine Publishers of America (MPA)
919 Third Avenue
New York, NY 10022
Tel: 212-872-3700
http://www.magazine.org

This organization offers student memberships for those interested in opinion writing.
National Conference of Editorial Writers
3899 North Front Street
Harrisburg, PA 17110
Tel: 717-703-3015
Email: ncew@pa-news.org
http://www.ncew.org

For information about working as a writer and union membership, contact
National Writers Union
113 University Place, 6th Floor
New York, NY 10003
Tel: 212-254-0279
Email: nwu@nwu.org
http://www.nwu.org

This organization for journalists has campus and online chapters.
Society of Professional Journalists
Eugene S. Pulliam National Journalism Center
3909 North Meridian Street
Indianapolis, IN 46208
Tel: 317-927-8000
http://www.spj.org

Contact this organization for information on film criticism in broadcasting.
Broadcast Film Critics Association
Email: info@bfca.org
http://www.bfca.org

The following organizations represent film critics in cities across the United States.
Chicago Film Critics Association
Email: contact@chicagofilmcritics.org
http://www.chicagofilmcritics.org

Los Angeles Film Critics Association
http://www.lafca.net

New York Film Critics Circle
http://www.nyfcc.com

The OFCS is an international association of Internet-based film critics and journalists.
Online Film Critics Society (OFCS)
Email: admissions@ofcs.org
http://ofcs.rottentomatoes.com

Lighting Technicians

OVERVIEW

Lighting technicians set up and control lighting equipment for motion pictures, television broadcasts, taped television shows, and video productions. They begin by consulting with the production director and technical director to determine the types of lighting and special effects that are needed. Working with spot and floodlights, mercury vapor lamps, white and colored lights, reflectors (mainly employed out-of-doors), and a large array of dimming, masking, and switching controls, they light scenes to be broadcast or recorded.

HISTORY

For centuries before the arrival of electric lights, theaters used candles and oil lamps to make the action on an indoor stage visible. The effects produced were necessarily limited by the lack of technology. In 1879, Thomas A. Edison developed a practical electric lightbulb by removing most of the oxygen from a glass bulb and then sending current through a carbon filament inside—producing a light that would not burn out. With the arrival of electric lights, it was only a short time before theater lighting became more sophisticated; spotlights and various lighting filters were put to use, and specialists in lighting emerged.

The manipulation of light and shadow is one of the basic principles of filmmaking. This was particularly the case during the era of the silent film; without sound, filmmakers relied upon images to tell their stories. Lighting professionals learned how to make the illusion complete; through expert lighting, cardboard backdrops could substitute for the outdoors, actors could change appearance, and cheaply constructed costumes could look extravagant. Lighting technicians were the first visual effects masters, using tricks with light to achieve realism. As film techniques and equipment evolved, lighting technicians worked with cinematographers and directors to create the dark recesses and gritty streets of the film noir, the lavish spectacle of the movie musical, and the sweeping plains of the American western, often within the confines of a studio. In the 1960s and 1970s, however, a new movie realism called for lighting technicians to expose, with uneven lighting and weak light sources, all the imperfections they'd been covering up before. Today, in the era of the special effects blockbuster, lighting technicians have gone back to their roots, using light and advanced equipment to make model cities, planets, and monsters look real.

THE JOB

Whenever a movie or television show is filmed, the location must be well lit, whether indoors in a studio or outdoors on location. Without proper lighting, the cameras would not be able to film properly, and the show would be difficult to watch. Lighting technicians set up and control the lighting equipment for movie and television productions. These technicians are sometimes known as *assistant chief set electricians* or *lights operators*.

When beginning a project, lighting technicians consult with the director to determine the lighting effects needed; then they arrange the lighting equipment and plan the light-switching sequence that will achieve the desired effects. For example, if the script calls for sunshine to be streaming in through a window, they will set up lights to produce this effect. Other effects they may be asked to produce include lightning, the flash from an explosion, or the soft glow of a candlelit room.

For a television series, which uses a similar format for each broadcast, the lights often remain in one fixed position for every show. For a one-time production, such as a scene in a movie, the lights have to be physically set up according to the particular scene.

During filming, lighting technicians follow a script that they have marked or follow instructions from the technical director. The script tells them which lighting effects are needed at every point in the filming. In a television studio, lighting technicians watch a monitor screen to check the lighting effects. If necessary they may alter the lighting as the scene progresses by adjusting controls in the control room.

Broadcasts from indoor settings require carrying and setting up portable lights. In small television stations, this work may be done by the camera operator or an assistant. In a large station, or in any big movie or television production, a lighting technician may supervise several assistants as they set up the lights.

Even outdoor scenes require lighting, especially to remove shadows from people's faces. For outdoor scenes in bad weather or on rough terrain, it may be a difficult task to secure the lighting apparatus firmly so that it is out of the way, stable, and protected. During a scene, whether broadcast live or recorded on film, lighting technicians must be able to concentrate on the lighting of the scene and must be able to make quick, sure decisions about lighting changes.

There are different positions within this field, depending on experience. A lighting technician can move up into the position of *best boy* (the term applies to both genders). This person assists the *chief lighting technician,* or *gaffer.* The gaffer is the head of the lighting department and hires the lighting crew. Gaffers must be sure the filmed scene looks the way the director and the director of photography want it to look. They must diagram each scene to be filmed and determine where to position each light and decide what kinds of lights will work best for each particular scene. Gaffers must be observant, noticing dark and bright spots and correcting their light levels before filming takes place.

REQUIREMENTS
High School
You should learn as much as possible about electronics in high school. Physics, mathematics, and any shop courses that introduce electronics equipment provide a good background. You should also take courses that will help you develop computer skills needed for operating lighting and sound equipment. Composition or technical writing courses can give you the writing skills you'll need to communicate ideas to other technicians.

Postsecondary Training
There is strong competition for motion picture and broadcast technician positions, and, in general, only well-prepared technicians get good jobs. You should attend a two-year postsecondary training program in electronics and broadcast technology, especially if you hope to advance to a supervisory position. Film schools also offer useful degrees in production, as do theater schools. For a position as a chief engineer, a bachelor's degree is usually required.

Other Requirements
Setting up lights can be taxing work, especially when lighting a large movie set. You should be able to handle heavy lights on stands and

work with suspended lights while on a ladder. Repairs such as changing light bulbs or replacing worn wires are sometimes necessary. You should be able to work with electricians' hand tools (screwdrivers, pliers, and so forth) and be comfortable working with electricity. You should also be dependable and capable of working as part of a team. Communications skills, both listening and speaking, are necessary when working with a director and with assistant light technicians.

EXPLORING

Valuable learning experiences for prospective lighting technicians include working on the lighting for a school stage production, building a radio from a kit, or a summer job in an appliance or TV or computer repair shop. High school shop or vocational teachers may be able to arrange a presentation by a qualified lighting technician.

You can also learn a lot about the technical side of production by operating a camera for your school's journalism or media department. Videotaping a play, concert, or sporting event will give you additional insight into production work. You may also have the opportunity to intern or volunteer with a local technical crew for a film or TV production. Check the Internet for production schedules, or volunteer to work for your state's film commission where you'll hear about area projects.

EMPLOYERS

Many lighting technicians work on a freelance basis, taking on film, TV, and commercial projects as they come along. Technicians can find full-time work with large theater companies and television broadcast stations, or any organization, such as a museum or sports arena, that requires special lighting. Lighting technicians also work for video production companies.

STARTING OUT

The best way to get experience is to find a position as an intern. Offering to work for a production for course credit or experience instead of pay will enable you to learn about the job and to establish valuable connections. Most people interested in film and television enter the industry as production assistants. These positions are often unpaid and require a great deal of time and work with little reward. However, production assistants have the opportunity to network with people in the industry. They get to speak to lighting technicians and to see them at work. Once they've worked on a few productions and have learned many of the basics of lighting, they can negotiate for paid positions on future projects.

ADVANCEMENT

An experienced lighting technician will be able to move up into the position of best boy. With a few more years' experience working under different gaffers on diverse projects, the technician may move into the position of gaffer or chief lighting technician. Gaffers command greater salaries as they gain experience working with many different cinematographers. Many experienced technicians join the International Alliance of Theatrical Stage Employees, Moving Picture Technicians, Artists and Allied Crafts of the United States, Its Territories and Canada (IATSE) as lighting technicians or studio mechanics; union membership is required for work on major productions. Some lighting technicians go on to work as cinematographers, or to make their own films or television movies.

EARNINGS

Salaries for lighting technicians vary according to the technician's experience. Annual income is also determined by the number of projects a technician is hired for; the most experienced technicians can work year-round on a variety of projects, while those starting out may go weeks without work. According to the IATSE, the minimum hourly pay for unionized gaffers was $22.50 in 2000. Unionized best boys and other lighting technicians earned at least $16.50 to $20.50 an hour. Experienced technicians can negotiate for much higher wages. Union members are also entitled to certain health and retirement benefits.

WORK ENVIRONMENT

Lighting technicians employed in television normally work a 40-hour week and change jobs only as their experience makes advancement possible. Technicians employed in the motion picture industry are often employed for one production at a time and thus may work less regularly and under a more challenging variety of conditions than light technicians in television studio work.

Technicians often work long days, especially when a film is on a tight schedule or when news teams are covering a late-breaking story. Technicians may travel a good deal to be on location for filming. They work both indoors in studios and outdoors on location, under a variety of weather conditions.

OUTLOOK

As long as the movie and television industries continue to grow, opportunities will remain available for people who wish to become lighting technicians. With the expansion of the cable market, lighting technicians may find work in more than one area. However, persistence and hard work are required in order to secure a good job in film or television.

The increasing use of visual effects and computer-generated imagery (CGI) will likely have an impact on the work of lighting technicians. Through computer programs, filmmakers and editors can adjust lighting themselves; however, live-action shots are still integral to the filmmaking process, and will remain so for some time. To get the initial shots of a film will require sophisticated lighting equipment and trained technicians. Lighting technicians often have to know about the assembly and operation of more pieces of equipment than anyone else working on a production. Equipment will become more compact and mobile, making the technician's job easier.

FOR MORE INFORMATION

For information about colleges with film and television programs of study, and to read interviews with filmmakers, visit the AFI website.
American Film Institute (AFI)
2021 North Western Avenue
Los Angeles, CA 90027
Tel: 323-856-7600
http://www.afi.com

Visit the ASC website for a great deal of valuable insight into the industry, including interviews with award-winning cinematographers, a "tricks of the trade" page, information about film schools, multimedia presentations, and the American Cinematographer *online magazine.*
American Society of Cinematographers (ASC)
PO Box 2230
Hollywood, CA 90078
Tel: 800-448-0145
Email: info@theasc.com
http://www.theasc.com

For education and training information, check out the following website:

International Alliance of Theatrical Stage Employees, Moving Picture Technicians, Artists and Allied Crafts of the United States, Its Territories and Canada
1430 Broadway, 20th Floor
New York, NY 10018
Tel: 212-730-1770
http://www.iatse-intl.org

Producers

QUICK FACTS

School Subjects
Business
English

Personal Skills
Communication/ideas
Leadership/management

Work Environment
Primarily indoors
Primarily one location

Minimum Education Level
High school diploma

Salary Range
$26,320 to $99,160 to
$200,000+

Certification or Licensing
None available

Outlook
About as fast as the average

DOT
187

GOE
01.01.01

NOC
5121

O*NET-SOC
27-2012.00

OVERVIEW

Producers organize and secure the financial backing for the production of motion pictures. They decide which scripts will be used or which books will be adapted for film. Producers also raise money to finance the filming of a motion picture; hire the director, screenwriter, and cast; oversee the budget and production schedule; and monitor the distribution of the film. Approximately 1,700 motion picture, television, and new media producers are members of the Producers Guild of America.

HISTORY

Motion picture cameras were invented in the late 1800s. The two earliest known films, made in 1888 by French-born Louis Le Prince, showed his father-in-law's garden and traffic crossing an English bridge.

More advanced cameras and motion picture techniques quickly followed. In 1903 American director Edwin Porter and inventor Thomas Edison made *The Great Train Robbery*, one of the first movies in which scenes were filmed out of sequence; when the filming was completed, the scenes were edited and spliced together. By 1906 feature-length films were being made and many talented and financially savvy individuals were making their livings as producers. The first woman to become a producer was Alice Guy, who started the Solax Company in New York in 1910.

In 1911 the Centaur Company, which had been trying to film westerns in New Jersey, moved to California and became the first studio to settle in Hollywood. Many film companies followed the lead of Centaur and moved their operations to southern California where there was abundant sunshine and a variety of terrain.

The film industry began to consolidate in the late 1920s after the introduction of sound films and the 1929 stock market crash. Small and marginally profitable producers were forced out of business, leaving the largest companies, which controlled most of the first-run theaters, to dominate the market. Major studios produced their films in a factory-like fashion. With their permanent staff of cameramen and other technical workers, a major studio could produce 40 or more films annually. And because many of the larger studios also owned their own network of theaters throughout the United States, they had a guaranteed market to which they could distribute their films. This stable, mass-produced system gave some studios the encouragement to produce commercially risky art films as well.

The introduction of television after World War II brought mixed fortunes to motion picture producers. Television was partly responsible for a decline in the number of theater goers, causing financial difficulties for the studios. An antitrust court judgment against the studios also eliminated their dominance of the movie theater market. But with the emergence and growth of television, and a steady need for new shows and made-for-TV films, television broadened employment opportunities for producers.

The major studios experienced financial difficulties in the 1950s, which because of studio downsizing and other pressures, led to a growth in the number of independent producers. Changes in the U.S. tax code made independent producing even more profitable. In response to their financial difficulties, studios began to reduce the number of films produced each year and to rely more on expensive "blockbuster" films to attract audiences.

In the early 1970s the industry again went through a major reorganization. The staggering expense of producing blockbusters had drained the major studios of their profits, and these financially strapped companies began to make films under strict cost-containment measures. Film projects, moreover, were increasingly initiated by independent producers.

Technical innovations have had great influence on motion picture producing. Portable lights, cameras, and other equipment allow films to be made anywhere and reduce the dependence on studio sets. More recently, the emergence of cable television and the ensuing demand for new shows has opened a new market for film producers. In recent years, the traditional distinctions between television and movie production, as well as between American and foreign films, have become increasingly blurred. Many foreign-made films are now financed by Americans, and a number of American motion picture companies are owned by foreigners.

THE JOB

The primary role of a producer is to organize and secure the financial backing necessary to undertake a motion picture project. The director, by contrast, creates the film from the screenplay. Despite this general distinction, the producer often takes part in creative decisions, and occasionally one person is both the producer and director. On some small projects, such as a nature or historical documentary for a public television broadcast, the producer might also be the writer and cameraman.

The job of a producer generally begins in the preproduction stage of filmmaking with the selection of a movie idea from a script, or other material. Some films are made from original screenplays, while others are adapted from books. If a book is selected, the producer must first purchase the rights from the author or his or her publishing company, and a writer must be hired to adapt the book into a screenplay format. Producers are usually inundated with scripts from writers and others who have ideas for a movie. Producers may have their own ideas for a motion picture and will hire a writer to write the screenplay. Occasionally a studio will approach a producer, typically a producer who has had many commercially or artistically successful films in the past, with a project.

After selecting a project, the producer will find a director, the technical staff, and the star actor or actors to participate in the film. Along with the script and screenwriter, these essential people are referred to as the package. Packaging is sometimes arranged with the help of talent agencies. It is the package that the producer tries to sell to an investor to obtain the necessary funds to finance the salaries and cost of the film.

There are three common sources for financing a film: major studios, production companies, and individual investors. A small number of producers have enough money to pay for their own projects. Major studios are the largest source of money, and finance most of the big budget films. Although some studios have full-time producers on staff, they hire self-employed, or *independent producers*, for many projects. Large production companies often have the capital resources to fund projects that they feel will be commercially successful. On the smaller end of the scale, producers of documentary films commonly approach individual donors; foundations; art agencies of federal, state, and local governments; and even family members and churches and other religious organizations. The National Endowment for the Humanities and the National Endowment for the Arts are major federal benefactors of cinema.

Raising money from individual investors can occupy much of the producer's time. Fund-raising may be done on the telephone, as well as in conferences, business lunches, and even cocktail parties. The producer may also look for a distributor for the film even before the production begins.

Obtaining the necessary financing does not guarantee a film will be made. After raising the money, the producer takes the basic plan of the package and tries to work it into a developed project. The script may be rewritten several times, the full cast of actors is hired, salaries are negotiated, and logistical problems, such as the location of the filming, are worked out; on some projects it might be the director who handles these tasks, or the director may work with the producer. Most major film projects do not get beyond this complicated stage of development.

During the production phase, the producer tries to keep the project on schedule and the spending within the established budget. Other production tasks include the review of dailies, which are prints of the day's filming. As the head of the project, the producer is ultimately responsible for resolving all problems, including personal conflicts such as those between the director and an actor and the director and the studio. If the film is successfully completed, the producer monitors its distribution and may participate in the publicity and advertising of the film.

To accomplish the many and varied tasks that the position requires, producers hire a number of subordinates, such as *associate producers*, sometimes called *coproducers, line producers,* and *production assistants.* Job titles, however, vary from project to project. In general, associate producers work directly under the producer and over see the major areas of the project, such as the budget. Line producers handle the day-to-day operations of the project. Production assistants may perform substantive tasks, such as reviewing scripts, but others are hired to run errands. Another title, *executive producer,* often refers to the person who puts up the money, such as a studio executive, but it is sometimes an honorary title with no functional relevance to the project.

REQUIREMENTS

There is no minimum educational requirement for becoming a producer. Many producers, however, are college graduates, and many also have a business degree or other previous business experience. They must not only be talented salespeople and administrators but

Interesting College Program

Interested in learning how to become a producer by attending college? If so, the Producers Program at the University of California-Los Angeles's School of Theater, Film, and Television might be a good place to start. Its faculty consists of respected producers, studio executives, agents, lawyers, and others involved in the motion picture and television industries. What type of classes do students involved in the program take? The following is a list of recent courses offered by the program:

- Producing the Trailer
- Feature Film Marketing
- New Technologies for the Independent Producer
- International Financing/Co-Production
- Entertainment Law and Business Practices
- Life After the Studio System
- The Independent Spirit: Creative Strategies
- Entertainment Management: What Makes a Hit
- Sports Entertainment
- Producing Boot Camp
- Producing TV Dramas
- Special Studies: Who Really Represents Me

For more information on the program, contact
University of California-Los Angeles
School of Theater, Film, and Television
Producers Program
102 East Melnitz Hall, Box 951622
Los Angeles, CA 90095-1622
Tel: 310-825 5761
http://www.tft.ucla.edu/producers/start.htm

also have a thorough understanding of films and motion picture technology. Such understanding, of course, only comes from experience.

High School

High school courses that will be of assistance to you in your work as a producer include speech, mathematics, business, psychology, and English.

Postsecondary Training

Formal study of film, television, communications, theater, writing, English literature, or art is helpful, as the producer must have the background to know whether an idea or script is worth pursuing. Many entry-level positions in the film industry are given to people who have studied liberal arts, cinema, or both.

In the United States there are more than a 1,000 colleges, universities, and trade schools that offer classes in film or television studies; more than 120 of these offer undergraduate programs, and more than 50 grant master's degrees. A small number of Ph.D. programs also exist.

The University of California-Los Angeles's School of Theater, Film, and Television offers a graduate-level Producers Program for students interested in careers in the film and television industries. Visit http://www.tft.ucla.edu/producers/start.htm for more information.

Graduation from a film or television program does not guarantee employment in the industry. Some programs are quite expensive, costing more than $50,000 in tuition alone for three years of study. Others do not have the resources to allow all students to make their own films.

Programs in Los Angeles and New York, the major centers of the entertainment industry, may provide the best opportunities for making contacts that can be of benefit when seeking employment.

Other Requirements

Producers come from a wide variety of backgrounds. Some start out as magazine editors, business school graduates, actors, or secretaries, messengers, and production assistants for a film studio. Many have never formally studied film.

Most producers, however, get their position through several years of experience in the industry, perseverance, and a keen sense for what projects will be artistically and commercially successful.

EXPLORING

There are many ways to gain experience in filmmaking. Some high schools have film and video clubs, for example, or courses on the use of motion picture equipment. Experience in high school or college theater can also be useful. One of the best ways to get experience is to volunteer for a student or low budget film project; positions on such projects are often advertised in local trade publications. Community cable stations also hire volunteers and may even offer internships.

EMPLOYERS

Many producers in the field are self-employed. Others are salaried employees of film companies, television networks, and television stations. Approximately 1,700 motion picture, television, and new media producers are members of the Producers Guild of America. The greatest concentration of motion picture producers is in Hollywood and New York City.

STARTING OUT

Becoming a producer is similar to becoming president of a company. Unless a person is independently wealthy and can finance whichever projects he or she chooses, prior experience in the field is necessary. Because there are so few positions, even with experience it is extremely difficult to become a successful producer.

Most motion picture producers have attained their position only after years of moving up the industry ladder. Thus, it is important to concentrate on immediate goals, such as getting an entry-level position in a film company. Some enter the field by getting a job as a production assistant. An entry-level production assistant may make copies of the scripts for actors to use, assist in setting up equipment, or may perform other menial tasks, often for very little or even no pay. While a production assistant's work is often tedious and of little seeming reward, it nevertheless does expose one to the intricacies of filmmaking and, more importantly, creates an opportunity to make contacts with others in the industry.

Those interested in the field should approach film companies, television stations, or the television networks about employment opportunities as a production assistant. Small television stations often provide the best opportunity for those who are interested in television producing. Positions may also be listed in trade publications.

ADVANCEMENT

There is little room for advancement because producers are at the top of their profession. Advancement for producers is generally measured by the types of projects they do, increased earnings, and respect in the field. At television stations, a producer can advance to program director. Some producers become directors or make enough money to finance their own projects.

EARNINGS

Producers are generally paid a percentage of the project's profits or a fee negotiated between the producer and a studio. The U.S. Department of Labor (USDL) reports that producers and directors earned average salaries of $52,840 in 2004. Salaries ranged from less than $26,320 to $87,980 or more. Producers of highly successful films can earn $200,000 or more, while those who make low-budget, documentary films might earn considerably less than the average. In general, producers in the film industry earn more than television producers. The USDL reports that producers employed in the motion picture industry had annual mean earnings of $99,160 in 2004, while those employed in television broadcasting averaged $54,400.

WORK ENVIRONMENT

Producers have greater control over their working conditions than most other people working in the motion picture industry. They may have the autonomy of choosing their own projects, setting their own hours, and delegating duties to others as necessary. The work often brings considerable personal satisfaction. But it is not without constraints. Producers must work within a stressful schedule complicated by competing work pressures and often daily crises. Each project brings a significant financial and professional risk. Long hours and weekend work are common. Most producers must provide for their own health insurance and other benefits.

OUTLOOK

Employment for producers is expected to grow about as fast as the average through 2012, according to the U.S. Department of Labor. Though opportunities may increase with the expansion of cable and satellite television, news programs, video and DVD rentals, and an increased overseas demand for American-made films, competition for jobs will be high. Live theater and entertainment will also provide job openings. Some positions will be available as current producers leave the workforce.

FOR MORE INFORMATION

For information on careers, contact
Producers Guild of America (PGA)
8530 Wilshire Boulevard, Suite 450
Beverly Hills, CA 90211
Tel: 310-358-9020
Email: info@producersguild.org
http://www.producersguild.org

Production Assistants

OVERVIEW

Production assistants perform a variety of tasks for film, television, and video producers and other staff members. They must be prepared to help out everywhere, ensuring that daily operations run as smoothly as possible. Some production assistants may perform substantive jobs, such as reviewing scripts, but others may primarily run errands. They must be willing to work hard and keep long hours at times, since tight production schedules require full days. An agreeable temperament and willingness to follow instructions and perform simple tasks are very important skills for work in this field.

HISTORY

In the early 20th century, as motion pictures were first developing, the roles of director and producer were combined in one person. European filmmakers such as Georges Melies and Leon Gaumont and New Yorker Edwin S. Porter directed, filmed, and produced very short movies. The first woman to become a director and producer was Alice Guy, who started the Solax Company in New York in 1910. The film industry settled in Hollywood and began to consolidate in the first two decades of this century, as jobs were differentiated. Major studios assembled large staffs, so all stages of production from conception to financing and directing could be performed within a single studio. Twentieth Century Fox, for example, would have producers, writers, directors, and actors on staff to choose from for each film. Small producers were forced out of business as major studios grew to have a monopoly on the industry.

In the 1950s the dominance of major studios in film production was curbed by an antitrust court decision, and more independent producers were able to find projects. Changes in the United States tax code made independent producing more profitable. At the same time, the growth of television provided new opportunities for producers, not only for television films, but news programs, weekly entertainment programs, sports broadcasts, talk shows, and documentaries. More recently, the video industry, particularly in the areas of music and education, has opened up even more production jobs.

The industry is becoming increasingly international; many foreign-made films and videos are now financed by Americans, and a number of American motion picture companies are under foreign ownership. Currently many producers work on a project-by-project basis. Independent producers must be good salespersons to market a project to a television or movie studio and to other financial backers. They will try to involve popular actors and media personalities with the project from its inception in order to attract a studio's interest. Studios hire production assistants to facilitate the work of the producer and other staff members.

THE JOB

The work of a production assistant is not glamorous, but production is the best place to learn about the film and television industries. All hiring, casting, and decision making is done by members of production; they are involved with a project from the very beginning through its final stages. The *producer* is in charge—he or she is responsible for coordinating the activities of all employees involved in a production. Producers oversee the budget, and they have the final word on most decisions made for a film or television show.

The responsibilities of production assistants (PAs) range from making sure the star has coffee in the morning to stopping street traffic so a director can film a scene. They photocopy the script for actors, assist in setting up equipment, and perform other menial tasks. The best PAs know where to be at the right time to make themselves useful. Production can be stressful; time is money and mistakes can be very costly. Assistants must be prepared to handle unforeseen problems, smooth out difficulties, and help out as quickly as possible.

Duties may include keeping production files in order. These files will include contracts, budgets, page changes (old pages from a script that has been revised), and other records. The documents must be kept organized and accessible for whenever the producer may need them.

Production assistants may also have to keep the producer's production folder in order and up-to-date. The production folder contains everything the producer needs to know about the production at a glance. It is particularly useful for times when a producer is on location away from the studio and cannot access the office files. PAs make sure that the folder includes the shooting schedule, the most recent version of the budget, cast and crew lists with phone numbers, a phone sheet detailing all production-related phone calls the producer needs to make, and the up-to-date shooting script. As new versions of these forms are created, PAs update the producer's folder and file the older versions for reference.

PAs may also be in charge of making sure that the producer gets the dailies, the film shot each day. They schedule an hour or so in a producer's schedule to watch the dailies and to make related calls to discuss them with other staff members.

PAs perform a number of other administrative and organizational tasks. They make travel reservations, arrange hotel accommodation, and arrange for rehearsal space. They run errands and communicate messages for producers, directors, actors, musicians, and other members of the technical crew.

PAs who work in television studios for live shows, such as news programs and talk shows, record news feeds, answer phones, operate teleprompters, coordinate tapes, and assist editors. They assist with booking guests and arranging interviews.

Production assistant is the lowest position on the film or television crew. It is an entry-level job that gives someone interested in film and broadcast media the experience and contacts to move into other areas of the industry. PAs often get stuck with undesirable tasks like sweeping floors, guarding sets, or finding a particular brand of green tea for a demanding diva. However, a film, television, or video production would not happen without production assistants on the set or in the studio.

REQUIREMENTS

High School

To work in the film or television industry, you should have an understanding of the artistic and technical aspects of production, as well as a broad knowledge of the industry itself. Take courses in photography, broadcast journalism, and media to learn about cameras and sound equipment. Take courses in art and art history to learn about visual composition, and English to develop communication skills.

Business and accounting courses can help you prepare for the book-keeping requirements of office work.

Postsecondary Training
There are no formal education requirements for production assistants. Most people in the industry consider the position a stepping stone into other careers in the industry. You'll learn much of what you'll need to know on the set of a film, following the instructions of crew members and other assistants. Though a film school education can't guarantee entry into the business, it can give you an understanding of the industry and help you make some connections. Many film students work part time or on a contract basis as production assistants to gain experience while they are still in school. There are more than 500 film studies programs offered by schools of higher education throughout the United States. According to the American Film Institute, the most reputable are: Columbia University in New York, New York University, the University of California at Los Angeles, and the University of Southern California. You may choose to major in English or theater as an undergraduate, then apply to graduate film schools. There are many good undergraduate programs in film and video with concentrations in such areas as directing, acting, editing, producing, screenwriting, cinematography, broadcast engineering, and television. Some people break into the business without formal training by volunteering on as many film productions as they can, getting to know professionals in the business, and making valuable connections in the industry. Your chances of moving up, however, are better if you have a college degree.

Other Requirements
Production assistants need agreeable personalities and a willingness to follow instructions and perform simple tasks. You need to catch on quickly to the things you're taught. Organizational skills will help you keep track of the many different aspects of a production. Great ambition and dedication are very important, as getting paying jobs on a production will require persistence. Also, you won't get a great deal of recognition for your hours of work, so you need a sense of purpose and an understanding that you are "paying your dues." A love of movies, video, and television and a fascination with the industry, particularly an interest in the technical aspects of filmmaking, will help you keep focused. Though you need an outgoing personality for making connections on a production, you should be capable of sitting quietly on the sidelines when not needed.

EXPLORING

There are many ways to gain experience with filmmaking. Some high schools have film clubs and classes in film or video. Experience in theater can also be useful. To learn more, you can work as a volunteer for a local theater or a low budget film project; these positions are often advertised in local trade publications. You may also be able to volunteer with your state's film commission, helping to solicit production companies to do their filming in the state.

Students interested in production work should read as much as possible about the film and television industry, starting at a school or public library. Trade journals can be very helpful as well; the two most prominent ones are *Daily Variety* (http://www.variety.com) and *Hollywood Reporter* (http://www.hollywoodreporter.com). These resources will have information about production studios that will prove very useful for prospective PAs. *The Rundown* (http://www.tvrundown.com) has information on the television news industry as well as career guidance information. If you are interested in video production, read *Studio/monthly* (http://www.avvideo.com).

EMPLOYERS

Production assistants are hired by film and video production companies for individual projects. Some assistants are employed full time in the main offices of a production company or as personal assistants to producers or executives. Production assistants can also find full-time employment at television studios.

STARTING OUT

Look for internships, which may offer course credit if they are unpaid, by reading trade journals and contacting film and television studios. You can also find production opportunities listed on the Internet or through your state's film commission. To gain experience, you may have to work for free on some of your first productions to make contacts within the industry. Since this is an entry-level position, opportunities will open as other assistants advance.

ADVANCEMENT

Production assistant positions are usually considered temporary. After one or two years, production assistants have enough experience to move into other jobs, and there are numerous choices, depending on their interests. They may wish to go into editing, camera operation, lighting, sound, writing, directing, producing, or performing. All of these areas have a hierarchy of positions that allow a production assistant to work his or her way up to the top jobs. A production assistant can, for example, become a *line producer,* who works closely with the producer, signing checks, advising on union rules, and negotiating deals with studio personnel. An *associate producer* performs similar work. To become a producer or director requires years of experience and hard work.

EARNINGS

Because working as a production assistant is the starting point for most professionals and artists in the film industry, many people volunteer their time until they make connections and move into paid positions. Those assistants who can negotiate payment may make between $200 and $400 a week, but they may only have the opportunity to work on a few projects a year. Production assistants working full time in an office may start at around $20,000 a year, but with experience can make around $65,000. Full-time production assistants may belong to the Office and Professional Employees International Union, which negotiates salaries. Experienced script supervisors, production office coordinators, and continuity coordinators have the opportunity to join Local #161 of the International Alliance of Theatrical Stage Employees, Moving Picture Technicians, Artists and Allied Crafts of the United States, Its Territories, and Canada. Its members may earn more than $180 a day when working for a production company.

According to Salary.com, production assistants earned a median annual salary of $24,763 in 2005. Salaries ranged from less than $19,812 to $31,023 or more annually.

Those working on a project-to-project basis won't receive any fringe benefits, but those employed full-time with a production company can expect health coverage and retirement benefits.

WORK ENVIRONMENT

A film set is an exciting environment, but the production assistant may be treated poorly there. With a positive attitude, energy, and a desire to be useful, PAs will earn respect from the production department.

There are unwritten rules that should be followed. A production assistant who works for the producer or for the studio can be seen as an outsider in the eyes of the director and the creative team, so PAs should be respectful and well-behaved. This means that production assistants should be quiet, stay out of the way, and avoid touching sets and equipment. If a production assistant behaves as a guest, but remains helpful when needed, he or she will earn a good reputation that will be valuable for his or her career advancement.

The work environment will vary; PAs may be required on location, or may work mainly in the studio. Production assistants must be willing to work long, demanding hours. Film productions are typically off schedule and over budget, requiring dedication from all those involved. Production assistants and other crew members often go days without seeing family members.

OUTLOOK

There will always be a need for assistants in film and television production. However, since it is such a good entry-level position for someone who wants to make connections and learn about the industry, competition for jobs can be tough. Fortunately, production assistants usually do not stay in their jobs more than one or two years, so turnover is fairly frequent. PAs will find employment anywhere a motion picture, television show, or video is being filmed, but significant opportunities exist in Los Angeles and New York—the production hubs of the industry. There may be opportunities at local television stations or smaller production companies that produce educational and corporate videos.

FOR MORE INFORMATION

For information about colleges with film and television programs of study, and to read interviews with filmmakers, visit the AFI website.
American Film Institute (AFI)
2021 North Western Avenue
Los Angeles, CA 90027-1657
Tel: 323-856-7600
http://www.afi.com

Visit the ASC website for a great deal of valuable insight into the industry, including interviews with award-winning cinematographers, information about film schools, multimedia presentations, and the American Cinematographer *online magazine.*
American Society of Cinematographers (ASC)
PO Box 2230
Hollywood, CA 90078

Tel: 800-448-0145
Email: info@theasc.com
http://www.theasc.com

For information about career publications, job listings, and industry statistics, contact
National Association of Broadcasters
1771 N Street, NW
Washington, DC 20036
Tel: 202-429-5300
Email: nab@nab.org
http://www.nab.org

For information about careers in cable TV, contact
National Cable and Telecommunications Association
1724 Massachusetts Avenue, NW
Washington, DC 20036
Tel: 202 775-3550
http://www.ncta.com

For information on careers, contact
Producers Guild of America
8530 Wilshire Boulevard, Suite 450
Beverly Hills, CA 90211
Tel: 310-358-9020
Email: info@producersguild.org
http://www.producersguild.org

Public Relations Specialists

OVERVIEW

Public relations (PR) specialists develop and maintain programs that present a favorable public image for an individual or organization. They provide information to the target audience (generally, the public at large) about the client, its goals and accomplishments, and any further plans or projects that may be of public interest.

PR specialists may be employed by corporations, government agencies, nonprofit organizations—almost any type of organization. Many PR specialists hold positions in public relations consulting firms or work for advertising agencies. There are approximately 158,000 public relations specialists in the United States.

HISTORY

The first public relations counsel was a reporter named Ivy Ledbetter Lee, who in 1906 was named press representative for coal mine operators. Labor disputes were becoming a large concern of the operators, and they had run into problems because of their continual refusal to talk to the press and the hired miners. Lee convinced the mine operators to start responding to press questions and supply the press with information on the mine activities.

During and after World War II, the rapid advancement of communications techniques prompted firms to realize they needed professional help to ensure their messages were given proper public attention. Manufacturing firms that had turned their production facilities over to the war effort returned to the manufacture of peace-time products and enlisted the aid of public relations professionals to forcefully bring products and the company name before the buying public.

Large business firms, labor unions, and service organizations, such as the American Red Cross, Boy Scouts of America, and the YMCA, began to recognize the value of establishing positive, healthy relationships with the public that they served and depended on for support. The need for effective public relations was often emphasized when circumstances beyond a company's or institution's control created unfavorable reaction from the public.

Public relations specialists must be experts at representing their clients before the media. The rapid growth of the public relations field since 1945 is testimony to the increased awareness in all industries of the need for professional attention to the proper use of media and the proper public relations approach to the many publics of a firm or an organization—customers, employees, stockholders, contributors, and competitors.

THE JOB

Public relations specialists are employed to do a variety of tasks. They may be employed primarily as writers, creating reports, news releases, and booklet texts. Others write speeches or create copy for radio, TV, or film sequences. These workers often spend much of their time contacting the press, radio, and TV as well as magazines on behalf of the employer. Some PR specialists work more as editors than writers, fact-checking and rewriting employee publications, newsletters, shareholder reports, and other management communications. Specialists may choose to concentrate in graphic design, using their background knowledge of art and layout for developing brochures, booklets, and photographic communications. Other PR workers handle special events, such as press parties, convention exhibits, open houses, or anniversary celebrations.

Public relations specialists employed by movie studios and television networks are concerned with efforts that will promote interest and create a buzz about their employer's movies or television shows. They work closely with their organization's marketing department to promote new movies, arrange print and broadcast interviews with the movie's stars or director, and undertake any other method of publicity that will encourage people to watch the movie or television show.

Many PR workers act as consultants (rather than staff) of a company (such as a movie studio or an independent production company), association, college, hospital, or other institution. These workers have the advantage of being able to operate independently, state opinions objectively, and work with more than one type of business or association.

PR specialists are called upon to work with the public opinion aspects of almost every corporate or institutional problem. In terms of the motion picture industry, this might include putting the best possible "spin" on an actor's controversial or unlawful behavior (such as a nightclub fight with paparazzi, a substance abuse problem, or offensive comments that the actor thought he or she was making off the record), explaining a studio's bargaining position during a strike by cinematographers, or detailing a production company's efforts to be environmentally friendly during filming in a pristine national park.

REQUIREMENTS

High School
While in high school, take courses in English, journalism, public speaking, humanities, and languages because public relations is based on effective communication with others. Courses such as these will develop your skills in written and oral communication as well as provide a better understanding of different fields and industries to be publicized.

Postsecondary Training
Most people employed in public relations have a college degree. Major fields of study most beneficial to developing the proper skills are public relations, English, and journalism. Some employers feel that majoring in the area in which the public relations person will eventually work is the best training. For example, if you are interested in working in the film or television industries, you might consider majoring in film or broadcasting. A knowledge of business administration is most helpful, as is an innate talent for selling. A graduate degree may be required for managerial positions. People with a bachelor's degree in public relations can find staff positions with either an organization or a public relations firm.

More than 200 colleges and about 100 graduate schools offer degree programs or special courses in public relations. In addition, many other colleges offer at least courses in the field. Public relations programs are sometimes administered by the journalism or communication departments of schools. In addition to courses in theory and techniques of public relations, interested individuals may study organization, management and administration, and practical applications and often specialize in areas such as business, government, and non-profit organizations. Other preparation includes courses in creative writing, psychology, communications, advertising, and journalism.

Certification or Licensing
The Public Relations Society of America and the International Association of Business Communicators accredit public relations workers who have at least five years of experience in the field and pass a comprehensive examination. Such accreditation is a sign of competence in this field, although it is not a requirement for employment.

Other Requirements
Today's public relations specialist must be a businessperson first, both to understand how to perform successfully in business and to comprehend the needs and goals of the organization or client. Additionally, the public relations specialist needs to be a strong writer and speaker, with good interpersonal, leadership, and organizational skills.

EXPLORING

Almost any experience in working with other people will help you to develop strong interpersonal skills, which are crucial in public relations. The possibilities are almost endless. Summer work on a newspaper or trade paper or with a television station or film company may give insight into communications media. Working as a volunteer on a political campaign can help you to understand the ways in which people can be persuaded. Being selected as a page for the U.S. Congress or a state legislature will help you grasp the fundamentals of government processes. A job in retail will help you to understand some of the principles of product presentation. A teaching job will develop your organization and presentation skills. These are just some of the jobs that will let you explore areas of public relations.

EMPLOYERS

Public relations specialists hold about 158,000 jobs. Workers may be paid employees of the organization they represent or they may be part of a public relations firm that works for organizations on a contract basis. Others are involved in fund-raising or political campaigning. Public relations may be done for a corporation, retail business, service company, utility, association, nonprofit organization, or educational institution.

Most PR firms are located in large cities that are centers of communications. New York, Chicago, San Francisco, Los Angeles, and Washington, D.C., are good places to start a search for a public relations job. Nevertheless, there are many good opportunities in cities across the United States.

STARTING OUT

There is no clear-cut formula for getting a job in public relations. Individuals often enter the field after gaining preliminary experience in another occupation closely allied to the field, usually some segment of communications, and frequently, in journalism. Coming into public relations from newspaper work is still a recommended route. Another good method is to gain initial employment as a public relations trainee or intern, or as a clerk, secretary, or research assistant in a public relations department or a consulting firm.

ADVANCEMENT

In some large companies, an entry-level public relations specialist may start as a trainee in a formal training program for new employees. In others, new employees may expect to be assigned to work that has a minimum of responsibility. They may assemble clippings or do rewrites on material that has already been accepted. They may make posters or assist in conducting polls or surveys, or compile reports from data submitted by others.

As workers acquire experience, they are given more responsibility. They write news releases, direct polls or surveys, or advance to writing speeches for company officials. Progress may seem to be slow, because some skills take a long time to master.

Some advance in responsibility and salary in the same firm in which they started. Others find that the path to advancement is to accept a more attractive position in another firm.

The goal of many public relations specialists is to open an independent office or to join an established consulting firm. To start an independent office requires a large outlay of capital and an established reputation in the field. However, those who are successful in operating their own consulting firms probably attain the greatest financial success in the public relations field.

EARNINGS

Public relations specialists employed in the motion picture and sound recording industries had mean annual earnings of $66,180 in 2004, according to the U.S. Department of Labor. Salaries for all public relations specialists ranged from less than $25,750 to more than $81,120.

Many PR workers receive a range of fringe benefits from corporations and agencies employing them, including bonus/incentive compensation, stock options, profit sharing/pension plans/401(k) programs, medical benefits, life insurance, financial planning, maternity/paternity leave, paid vacations, and family college tuition. Bonuses can range from 5 to 100 percent of base compensation and often are based on individual and/or company performance.

WORK ENVIRONMENT

Public relations specialists generally work in offices with adequate secretarial help, regular salary increases, and expense accounts. They are expected to make a good appearance in tasteful, conservative clothing. They must have social poise, and their conduct in their personal life is important to their firms or their clients. The public relations specialist may have to entertain business associates.

The PR specialist seldom works the conventional office hours for many weeks at a time; although the workweek may consist of 35 to 40 hours, these hours may be supplemented by evenings and even weekends when meetings must be attended and other special events covered. Time behind the desk may represent only a small part of the total working schedule. Travel is often an important and necessary part of the job.

The life of the PR worker is so greatly determined by the job that many consider this a disadvantage. Because the work is concerned with public opinion, it is often difficult to measure the results of performance and to sell the worth of a public relations program to an employer or client. Competition in the consulting field is keen, and if a firm loses an account, some of its personnel may be affected. The demands it makes for anonymity will be considered by some as one of the profession's less inviting aspects. Public relations involves much more hard work and a great deal less glamour than is popularly supposed.

OUTLOOK

Employment of public relations professionals is expected to grow faster than the average for all other occupations through 2012, according to the U.S. Department of Labor. Competition will be keen for beginning jobs in public relations because so many job seekers are enticed by the perceived glamour and appeal of the field; those with both education and experience will have an advantage.

Most large companies have some sort of public relations resource, either through their own staff or through the use of a firm of consultants. They are expected to expand their public relations activities and create many new jobs. More of the smaller companies are hiring public relations specialists, adding to the demand for these workers. Additionally, as a result of recent corporate scandals, more public relations specialists will be hired to help improve the images of companies and regain the trust of the public.

FOR MORE INFORMATION

For information on accreditation, contact
International Association of Business Communicators
One Hallidie Plaza, Suite 600
San Francisco, CA 94102-2818
Tel: 415-544-4700
http://www.iabc.com

For statistics, salary surveys, and information on accreditation and student membership, contact
Public Relations Society of America
33 Maiden Lane, 11th Floor
New York, NY 10038-5150
Tel: 212-460-1400
Email: prssa@prsa.org (student membership)
http://www.prsa.org

Screenwriters

OVERVIEW

Screenwriters write scripts for entertainment, education, training, sales, television, and films. They may choose themes themselves, or they may write on a theme assigned by a producer or director, sometimes adapting plays or novels into screenplays. Screenwriting is an art, a craft, and a business. It is a career that requires imagination and creativity, the ability to tell a story using both dialogue and pictures, and the ability to negotiate with producers and studio executives.

HISTORY

In 1894, Thomas Edison invented the kinetograph to take a series of pictures of actions staged specifically for the camera. In October of the same year, the first film opened at Hoyt's Theatre in New York. It was a series of acts performed by such characters as a strongman, a contortionist, and trained animals. Even in these earliest motion pictures, the plot or sequence of actions the film would portray was written down before filming began.

Newspaperman Roy McCardell was the first person to be hired for the specific job of writing for motion pictures. He wrote captions for photographs in a weekly entertainment publication. When he was employed by *Biograph* to write 10 scenarios, or stories, at $10 apiece, it caused a flood of newspapermen to try their hand at screenwriting.

The early films, which ran only about a minute and were photographs of interesting movement, grew into story films, which ran between nine and 15 minutes. The demand for original plots led to the development of story departments at each of the motion picture companies in the period from 1910 to 1915. The story departments were responsible for writing the stories and also for reading and evaluating material that came from outside sources. Stories usually came from writers, but some were purchased from actors on the lot. The actor Genevieve (Gene) Gauntier was paid $20 per reel of film for her first scenarios.

There was a continuing need for scripts because usually a studio bought a story one month, filmed the next, and released the film the month after. Some of the most popular stories in these early films were Wild West tales and comedies.

Longer story films began to use titles, and as motion pictures became longer and more sophisticated, so did the titles. In 1909–10, there was an average of 80 feet of title per 1,000 feet of film. By 1926, the average increased to 250 feet of title per 1,000 feet. The titles included dialogue, description, and historical background.

In 1920, the first Screen Writers Guild was established to ensure fair treatment of writers, and in 1927, the Academy of Motion Picture Arts and Sciences was formed, including a branch for writers. The first sound film, *The Jazz Singer,* was also produced in 1927. Screenwriting changed dramatically to adapt to the new technology.

From the 1950s to the 1980s, the studios gradually declined, and more independent film companies and individuals were able to break into the motion picture industry. The television industry began to thrive in the 1950s, further increasing the number of opportunities for screenwriters. During the 1960s, people began to graduate from the first education programs developed specifically for screenwriting.

Today, most Americans have spent countless hours viewing programs on television and movie screens. Familiarity with these mediums has led many writers to attempt writing screenplays. This has created an intensely fierce marketplace with many more screenplays being rejected than accepted each year.

THE JOB

Screenwriters write dramas, comedies, soap operas, adventures, westerns, documentaries, newscasts, and training films. They may write original stories, or get inspiration from newspapers, magazines, books, or other sources. They may also write scripts for continuing television series. *Motion picture writers* submit an original screenplay or adaptation of a book to a motion picture producer or studio. *Continuity writers* in broadcasting create station announcements, previews of coming shows, and advertising copy for local sponsors. *Broadcasting scriptwriters* usually work in a team, writing for a certain audience, to fill a certain time slot. *Playwrights* submit their plays to drama companies for performance or try to get their work published in book form.

Screenwriters may work on a staff of writers and producers for a large company. Or they may work independently for smaller companies that hire only freelance production teams. Advertising agencies also hire writers, sometimes as staff, sometimes as freelancers.

Scripts are written in a two-column format, one column for dialogue and sound, the other for video instructions. One page of script equals about one minute of running time, though it varies. Each page has about 150 words and takes about 20 seconds to read. Screenwriters send a query letter outlining their idea before they submit a script to a production company. Then they send a standard release form and wait at least a month for a response. Studios buy many more scripts than are actually produced, and studios often will buy a script only with provisions that the original writer or another writer will rewrite it to their specifications.

REQUIREMENTS

High School
You can develop your writing skills in English, theater, speech, and journalism classes. Belonging to a debate team can also help you learn how to express your ideas within a specific time allotment and framework. History, government, and foreign language can contribute to a well-rounded education, necessary for creating intelligent scripts. Taking business courses can be useful in understanding basic business principles you will encounter in the film industry.

Postsecondary Training
There are no set educational requirements for screenwriters. A college degree is desirable, especially a liberal arts education, which exposes you to a wide range of subjects. An undergraduate or graduate film program will likely include courses in screenwriting, film theory, and other subjects that will teach you about the film industry and its history. A creative writing program will involve you with workshops and seminars that will help you develop fiction-writing skills.

Other Requirements
As a screenwriter, you must be able to create believable characters and develop a story. You must have technical skills, such as dialogue writing, creating plots, and doing research. In addition to creativity

And the Oscar Goes To . . .

The following screenwriters have won the Oscar for best original screenplay in the last decade:

2004: Charlie Kaufman for *Eternal Sunshine of the Spotless Mind*
2003: Sofia Coppola for *Lost in Translation*
2002: Pedro Almodovar for *Talk to Her*
2001: Julian Fellowes for *Gosford Park*
2000: Cameron Crowe for *Almost Famous*
1999: Alan Ball for *American Beauty*
1998: Marc Norman and Tom Stoppard for *Shakespeare In Love*
1997: Matt Damon and Ben Affleck for *Good Will Hunting*
1996: Ethan Coen and Joel Coen for *Fargo*
1995: Christopher McQuarrie for *The Usual Suspects*
1994: Quentin Tarantino and Roger Avary for *Pulp Fiction*

For more films by Academy Award-winning screenwriters, visit http://www.oscars.org/awardsdatabase.

and originality, you also need an understanding of the marketplace for your work. You should be aware of what kinds of scripts are in demand by producers. Word processing skills are also helpful.

EXPLORING

One of the best ways to learn about screenwriting is to read and study scripts. It is advisable to watch a motion picture while simultaneously following the script. The scripts for such classic films as *Casablanca, Network,* and *Chinatown* are often taught in college screenwriting courses. You should read film-industry publications, such as *Daily Variety* (http://www.variety.com), *Hollywood Reporter* (http://www.hollywoodreporter.com), and *The Hollywood Scriptwriter* (http://www.hollywoodscriptwriter.com). There are a number of books about screenwriting, but they're often written by those outside of the industry. These books are best used primarily for learning about the format required for writing a screenplay. There are also computer software programs that assist with screenplay formatting.

The Sundance Institute, a Utah-based production company, accepts unsolicited scripts from those who have read the institute's submission guidelines. Every January they choose a few scripts and invite the writers to a five-day program of one-on-one sessions with professionals. The process is repeated in June and also includes a videotaping of sections of chosen scripts. The institute doesn't produce features, but they can often introduce writers to those who do. (For contact information, see the end of this article.)

Most states offer grants for emerging and established screenwriters and other artists. Contact your state's art council for guidelines and application materials. In addition, several arts groups and associations hold annual contests for screenwriters. To find out more about screenwriting contests, consult a reference work such as *The Writer's Market* (http://www.writersmarket.com).

Students may try to get their work performed locally. A teacher may be able to help you submit your work to a local radio or television station or to a publisher of plays.

EMPLOYERS

Most screenwriters work on a freelance basis, contracting with production companies for individual projects. Those who work for television may contract with a TV production company for a certain number of episodes or seasons.

STARTING OUT

The first step to getting a screenplay produced is to write a letter to the script editor of a production company describing yourself, your training, and your work. Ask if the editors would be interested in reading one of your scripts. You should also pursue a manager or agent by sending along a brief letter describing a project you're working on. A list of agents is available from the Writers Guild of America (WGA). If you receive an invitation to submit more, you'll then prepare a synopsis, or treatment, of the screenplay, which is usually from one to 10 pages. It should be in the form of a narrative short story, with little or no dialogue.

Whether you are a beginning or experienced screenwriter, it is best to have an agent, since studios, producers, and stars often return unsolicited manuscripts unopened to protect themselves from plagiarism charges. Agents provide access to studios and producers, interpret contracts, and negotiate deals.

It is wise to register your script (online registration is $10 for members, $22 for nonmembers, and $17 for students) with the WGA. Although registration offers no legal protection, it is proof that on a specific date you came up with a particular idea, treatment, or script.

You should also keep a detailed journal that lists the contacts you've made, including the people who have read your script.

ADVANCEMENT

Competition is stiff among screenwriters, and a beginner will find it difficult to break into the field. More opportunities become available as a screenwriter gains experience and a reputation, but that is a process that can take many years. Rejection is a common occurrence in the field of screenwriting. Most successful screenwriters have had to send their screenplays to numerous production companies before they find one that likes their work.

Once they have sold some scripts, screenwriters may be able to join the WGA. Membership with the WGA guarantees the screenwriter a minimum wage for a production and other benefits such as arbitration. Some screenwriters, however, writing for minor productions, can have regular work and successful careers without WGA membership.

Those screenwriters who manage to break into the business can benefit greatly from recognition in the industry. In addition to creating their own scripts, some writers are also hired to "doctor" the scripts of others, using their expertise to revise scripts for production. If a film proves very successful, a screenwriter will be able to command higher payment, and will be able to work on high-profile productions. Some of the most talented screenwriters receive awards from the industry, most notably the Academy Award for best original or adapted screenplay.

EARNINGS

Wages for screenwriters are nearly impossible to track. Some screenwriters make hundreds of thousands of dollars from their scripts, while others write and film their own scripts without any payment at all, relying on backers and loans. Screenwriter Joe Eszterhas made entertainment news in the early 1990s when he received $3 million for each of his treatments for *Basic Instinct, Jade,* and *Showgirls.* In the early 2000s, many scripts by first-time screenwriters were sold for between $500,000 and $1 million. Typically, a writer will earn a percentage (approximately 1 percent) of the film's budget. Obviously, a lower budget film pays considerably less than a big production, starting at $15,000 or less. According to the WGA, the median income for WGA members was $87,104 in 2001. Earnings ranged from less than $28,091 to more than $567,726. Screenwriters who are WGA members also are eligible to receive health benefits. The U.S. Department of Labor reports that writers employed in the motion picture and video industries had mean earnings of $63,350 in 2004.

WORK ENVIRONMENT

Screenwriters who choose to freelance have the freedom to write when and where they choose. They must be persistent and patient; only one in 20 to 30 purchased or optioned screenplays is produced.

Screenwriters who work on the staff of a large company, for a television series, or under contract to a motion picture company may share writing duties with others.

Screenwriters who do not live in Hollywood or New York will likely have to travel to attend script conferences. They may even have to relocate for several weeks while a project is in production. Busy periods before and during film production are followed by long periods of inactivity and solitude. This forces many screenwriters, especially those just getting started in the field, to work other jobs and pursue other careers while they develop their talent and craft.

OUTLOOK

There is intense competition in the television and motion picture industries. There are approximately 11,000 members of the WGA. A 2001 report by the WGA found that only 50.7 percent of its members were actually employed the previous year. The report also focused on the opportunities for women and minority screenwriters. Despite employment for minority screenwriters substantially increasing, employment for women changed little in that decade. Eighty percent of those writing for feature films are white males. Though this domination in the industry will eventually change because of efforts by women and minority filmmakers, the change may be slow in coming. The success of independent cinema, which has introduced a number of women and minority filmmakers to the industry, will continue to contribute to this change.

As cable television expands and digital technology allows for more programming, new opportunities will emerge. Television networks continue to need new material and new episodes for long-running series. Studios are always looking for new angles on action, adventure, horror, and comedy, especially romantic comedy stories. The demand for new screenplays should increase slightly in the next decade, but the number of screenwriters is growing at a faster rate.

Writers will continue to find opportunities in advertising agencies and educational and training video production houses.

FOR MORE INFORMATION

This organization provides membership and resources to aspiring screenwriters. It offers career information, competitions, and a high school outreach program.

American Screenwriters Association
269 South Beverly Drive, Suite 2600
Beverly Hills, CA 90212-3807
Tel: 866-265-9091
http://www.asascreenwriters.com

For guidelines on submitting a script for consideration for the Sundance Institute's screenwriting program, send a self-addressed stamped envelope to the Institute or visit the following website:

Sundance Institute
8530 Wilshire Boulevard, 3rd Floor
Beverly Hills, CA 90211-3114
Tel: 310-360-1981
Email: la@sundance.org
http://institute.sundance.org

To learn more about the film industry, to read interviews and articles by noted screenwriters, and to find links to many other screenwriting-related sites on the Internet, visit the websites of the WGA.

Writers Guild of America (WGA)
East Chapter
555 West 57th Street, Suite 1230
New York, NY 10019
Tel: 212-767-7800
http://www.wgaeast.org

Writers Guild of America (WGA)
West Chapter
7000 West Third Street
Los Angeles, CA 90048
Tel: 800-548-4532
http://www.wga.org

Visit the following website to read useful articles on screenwriting
Screenwriters Utopia
http://www.screenwritersutopia.com

INTERVIEW

Michael Taav began his career as a playwright, theatre producer, and director. Ultimately, his focus turned toward film. He has spent the past 18 years working as a screenwriter, movie director, script consultant, and author. Currently, Dr. Taav is a film educator at Columbia College Chicago. He was kind enough to discuss his eclectic career with the editors of Careers in Focus: Film.

Q. How long have you been a film educator? What classes do you typically teach?

A. I've been teaching film for the past 10 years, first at the University of California-San Diego, then New York University, and more recently, at Columbia College. Among the courses I've taught are Introduction to Screenwriting, Advanced Screenwriting, Graduate Screenwriting, Script Analysis, Introduction to Genre, and Film Directing

Q. Tell us about your career in the film industry.

A. I began my career writing and directing plays. After having my works performed in Los Angeles, Chapel Hill, and a number of off-off-Broadway and off-Broadway theatres, I wrote my first screenplay, the short, *Tom Goes To The Bar. Tom* won the Golden Bear at the Berlin Film Festival, the Silver Prize at the Chicago Film Festival, The Certificate of Merit by the Melbourne Film Festival, and was critically praised by the *New York Times,* the *Los Angeles Times,* and the *Boston Globe.* As a result of *Tom's* success, I sold three feature screenplays the following year and was commissioned shortly thereafter to 1) write a *Tales From The Crypt* episode and 2) rewrite scripts for HBO, New Line Pictures, and Bio Films in Iceland.

In order to gain greater creative control over my screenplays, I decided to direct them. I applied for and was awarded a $70,000 production grant by Chanticleer Films and the Showtime Network, thereby enabling me to film my half-hour screenplay, *Hoggs' Heaven. Hoggs'* premiered on Showtime's *Thirty-Minute Film Festival* hosted by Rob Reiner. The next year I was hired by Columbia-Tri-Star to direct my feature script, *The Paint Job.* This film was awarded the Silver Prize in the Houston Film Festival Feature Competition and was subsequently shown at the Boston, London, Edinburgh, Cannes, and Norwegian Film Festivals. It received its theatrical premiere in London and was selected "Film of the Month" by the British humor magazine

Deadpan, and one of the "Best Five Films presently in release" by *Time-Out* magazine.

Since then, I've written the feature scripts, *Pandora,* for UTB Productions; *One Shot Deal,* for Parisot Productions; served as a script consultant on the studio films, *Home Fries* and *Galaxy Quest;* authored the critical text A *Body Across the Map: The Father-Son Plays of Sam Shepard;* and was honored with a two-day retrospective of my films by the University of New Hampshire. Presently, I am writing the feature script *Witch Hunt,* with the support of the Columbia College Department of Film and Video and the Dean and Provost of Media Arts.

Q. What are the most important qualities of a successful film in terms of writing and direction?

A. In terms of screenwriting, I'd define a successful film as one that has an insistent, unpredictable and yet plausible plot, and clearly individualized characters who elicit strong emotional responses (be they positive or negative). In regards to directing, I'd describe a successful film as one that maximizes the dramatic impact of the script, is visually and aurally inventive, effectively establishes its tone/mood, and is convincingly performed.

Q. What are the most important personal qualities for successful film and video majors?

A. In order for film and video majors to succeed professionally, they need be disciplined, conscientious, humble (i.e., willing to learn), patient, persistent, and capable of collaboration. Moreover, they should be certain that this is what they want to do with their lives. This conviction is absolutely essential if they are to weather the occasional difficulty or disappointment.

Q. What advice would you offer film and video majors as they graduate and try to break into the field?

A. My first recommendation would be for graduating film and video majors to move for at least a few years to where the majority of films, TV shows, commercials, and music videos are produced—meaning either New York or Los Angeles. I would also advise them not to come empty-handed. They should arrive with a list of professionals to contact as well as a completed short film, screenplay, and/or a creative reel. Furthermore, I believe they should accept almost any job that gets them "in the door," no matter how humble. Finally, I recommend that students continue to create stories and scripts that reflect their individual creative visions rather than churn out work that is conspicuously commercial (i.e., imitations of works that already exist).

Special Effects Technicians

OVERVIEW

Special effects technicians work to make the illusions in movies, theater, and television seem real. When a director wants us to see a man turn into a wolf or a train explode in a fiery crash, it is the job of special effects technicians to make it happen. They work with a variety of materials and techniques to produce the fantastic visions and seemingly real illusions that add dimension to a film.

HISTORY

At the turn of the century a French magician-turned-filmmaker named Georges Melies invented motion picture special effects. To film futuristic space flight in *A Trip to the Moon,* he made a model of a rocket and fired it from a cannon in front of a painted backdrop. By the 1920s, special effects, or "tricks," had become a department of the major film studios, and technicians were steadily inventing new techniques and illusions. For a tornado scene in *The Wizard of Oz,* a miniature house was filmed falling from the studio ceiling, and when the film was reversed it became Dorothy's house flying into the air. Effects departments still make extensive use of miniature models, which are easy to work with and save money.

In 1950 the Supreme Court broke up the movie studio monopolies. Independent, low-budget films began to proliferate and to affect audience tastes. They helped to make realistic, on-site shoots fashionable, and studio special effects departments became virtually extinct. It was not until the 1970s, when George Lucas brought his imagination and effects to *Star Wars*, that special effects were revived in force. The crew that Lucas assembled for that project formed the company Industrial Light & Magic (ILM), which still commands prestige in a field that now includes hundreds of large and small special effects companies. ILM is responsible for the effects in more than 100 feature films, including several of the top box office hits in movie history.

The industry toyed with computer-generated imagery (CGI) in the 1980s, with such films as *Tron* and *Star Trek II*. By the 1990s, the movie-going public was ready for an effects revolution, which began with James Cameron's *The Abyss* and *Terminator 2: Judgment Day* and reached full-force with 1993's *Jurassic Park. Twister* in 1996, *Titanic* in 1997, and *The Matrix* in 1999 raised the stakes for movie effects, and *Star Wars: Episode I—The Phantom Menace* used 2,000 digital shots (compared to *Titanic*'s 500). Digital inking and painting, along with a software program called Deep Canvas, gave Disney's *Tarzan* its great depth and dimension and detail unlike any other film in the history of animation. Today, computer-generated imagery, and the work of special effects technicians, play an integral role in the movie industry.

THE JOB

Special effects technicians are craftsmen who work in a variety of areas to provide seamless, illusionary effects for film, television, and stage productions. Their work is very creative; they read scripts and consult with the director to determine the kinds of effects that will be required. Often the director has only a general idea of what he or she wants; technicians come up with the artistic specifics and functional designs, and then create what they have designed.

There are several trades that make up special effects, and special effects companies, known as shops, may do business in one or several of these trades. The services they may offer include mechanical effects, computer animation, makeup effects, and pyrotechnics.

Mechanical effects specialists build the props, sets, and backdrops for film, television, and theater productions. They build, install, and operate equipment, working with a variety of materials depending on the effects required. They are usually skilled in several areas, including carpentry, welding, electricity, and robotics.

Computer animation specialists use computer programs to create effects that would be impossible or too costly to build otherwise. Computer animation/CGI has made advances into television commercials as well as film. These effects make it possible for a human face to transform or "morph" into an animal's, or for a realistic looking bear to drink from a soda can. Computer animation specialists typically

A special effects technician applies paint to a mask in his studio.
(Shelley Gazin, Corbis)

work in offices, not on location as other specialists do. They must be highly skilled with computers and keep abreast of new technology.

Makeup effects specialists create elaborate costumes and masks for actors to wear in movies or on stage. They also build prosthetic devices to simulate human or animal heads and limbs. They may be skilled at modeling, sewing, applying makeup, and mixing dyes.

Pyrotechnic effects specialists are experts with explosives and firearms. They create explosions for dramatic scenes. Their work can be very dangerous, and in most states they are required to be licensed in order to handle and set off explosives.

Specialists who are union members are contracted to provide a specific service and rarely work outside their area of expertise. Nonunion people may be required to help out with tasks that fall outside the union members' areas of expertise. This may involve constructing sets, moving heavy equipment, or helping with last-minute design changes.

REQUIREMENTS

High School
Special effects technicians rely on a mix of science and art. To prepare for this career, take all the art courses you can, including art history; many filmmakers look to classical art when composing shots

and lighting effects. Photography courses will help you understand the use of light and shadow. Chemistry can give you some insight into the products you will be using. To work with computer animation, you should have an understanding of the latest graphics programs.

Postsecondary Training
While there are no formal educational requirements for becoming a special effects technician, some universities have film and television programs that include courses in special effects. Some special effects technicians major in theater, art history, photography, and related subjects. Many colleges and universities offer masters of fine arts degrees. These are studio programs in which you will be able to gain hands-on experience in theater production and filmmaking with a faculty composed of practicing artists. Some of the CGI technicians working today have not had any special schooling or training, having mastered graphics programs on their own.

Certification or Licensing
To work as a pyrotechnics specialist, most states require you to be licensed to handle explosives and firearms.

Other Requirements
Special effects work is physically and mentally demanding. Technicians must be able to work as members of a team, following instructions carefully in order to avoid dangerous situations. They often work long days, so they must possess stamina. In addition, the work on a set can be uncomfortable; a mechanical effects specialist may have to work under adverse weather conditions or wait patiently in a small space for the cue to operate an effect. Freelance technicians will often have to provide their own tools and equipment, which they either own or rent, when hired for a job.

Computer animation specialists may sit for long hours in front of a computer, performing meticulous and sometimes repetitive work. Makeup effects specialists spend most of their time working in a trailer on the set or in a shop where they construct and adjust the items required by the actors. Special effects technicians must work both carefully and quickly; a mistake or a delay can become very expensive for the production company.

EXPLORING
Students who like to build things, or who tend to be curious about how things work, might be well suited to a career in special effects. To learn

more about the profession, visit your school or public library and bookstores to read more about the field. Browse magazine racks to find Hollywood trade magazines and other related material on your area of interest; *Animation Journal* (http://www.animationjournal.com), *Animation World* (http://mag.awn.com), *Cinefex* (http://www.cinefex.com), *Daily Variety* (http://www.variety.com), and *Hollywood Reporter* (http://www.hollywoodreporter.com) are good places to start.

You might also consider becoming a member of S.C.R.E.A.M—the Student Club of Realistic Effects, Animatronics, and Makeup, a network of students of all ages who share interest in special effects and the film industry. Its website (http://www.geocities.com/Hollywood/Lot/9373/SCREAM/scream.html) features a chat room, a list of training programs, a glossary, and a message board that includes postings on making sugar glass, working with explosions and zombies, and fashioning your own homemade "squibs" (devices worn by actors that explode with fake blood to simulate taking a bullet).

Since experience and jobs are difficult to get in the film and television industry, it is important to learn about the career to be sure it is right for you. Working on high school drama productions as a stagehand, "techie," or makeup artist can be helpful for learning set and prop design, methods of handling equipment, and artistry. Community theaters and independent filmmakers can provide volunteer work experience; they rely on volunteers because they have limited operating funds.

Alternatively, if you find you are adept in computer classes and curious about advances in computer animation, you may wish to pursue this field by continuing your learning and exploration of computer techniques.

EMPLOYERS

The top special effects technicians work for special effects houses. These companies contract with individual film productions; one film may have the effects created by more than one special effects company. ILM is the top company, having done the effects for such films as *Star Wars: Episode I, Harry Potter & the Sorcerer's Stone,* and *War of the Worlds.* Other major companies include Digital Domain (*Titanic, Lord of the Rings: The Fellowship of the Ring,* and *I, Robot*) and Giant Killer Robots or GKR (*Terminator 3: Rise of the Machines, What Dreams May Come,* and *Fantastic Four*). Some special effects technicians own their own effects company or work on a freelance basis. Freelance technicians may work in several areas, doing theater work, film and television productions, and commercials.

STARTING OUT

Internships are a very good way to gain experience and make your-self a marketable job candidate. Film and theater companies are pre-dominantly located in Los Angeles or New York, but there are opportunities elsewhere. Again, since theater and lower budget film productions operate with limited funds, you could find places to work for course credit or experience instead of a salary.

Special effects shops are excellent places to try for an internship. You may find them in books and trade magazines, or try the yellow pages under theatrical equipment, theatrical makeup, and theatrical and stage lighting equipment. Even if one shop has no opportunities, it may be able to provide the name of another that takes interns.

You should keep a photographic record of all the work you do for theater and film productions, including photos of any drawings or sculptures you have done for art classes. It is important to have a port-folio or demo reel (a reel of film demonstrating your work) to send along with your resume to effects shops, makeup departments, and producers.

Special effects technicians may choose to join a union; some film studios will only hire union members. The principal union for spe-cial effects technicians is the International Alliance of Theatrical Stage Employees, Moving Picture Technicians, Artists of the Allied Trades of the United States, Its Territories and Canada (IATSE). To get into the union, a technician must complete a training program, which includes apprenticing in a prop-making shop and passing an examination. Union members work under a union contract that determines their work rules, pay, and benefits.

ADVANCEMENT

Good special effects technicians will acquire skills in several areas, becoming versatile and therefore desirable employees. Since many work on a freelance basis, it is useful to develop a good reputation and maintain contacts from past jobs. Successful technicians may be chosen to work on increasingly prestigious and challenging produc-tions. Once they have a strong background and diverse experience, technicians may start their own shops.

EARNINGS

Some technicians have steady, salaried employment, while others work freelance for an hourly rate and may have periods with no work. The average daily rate for beginning technicians is $100 to $200 per day, while more experienced technicians can earn $300 per day or more. A member salary survey conducted by IATSE shows that employment in digital effects can pay very well, even in assistant positions. When adjusted to show annual figures, the survey found that character animators, CGI effects animators, and art directors had median yearly earnings of around $100,000. On the low end of the scale, these professionals earned around $55,000, and on the high end, $350,000. Effects assistants had beginning wages of around $45,000, and median wages of $60,000.

Those working freelance will not have the benefits of full-time work, having to provide their own health insurance. Those working for special effects houses have the usual benefit packages including health insurance, bonuses, and retirement.

WORK ENVIRONMENT

Special effects is an excellent field for someone who likes to dream up fantastic monsters and machines and has the patience to create them. Special effects technicians must be willing to work long hours and have the stamina to work under strenuous conditions. Twelve-hour days are not uncommon, and to meet a deadline technicians may work for 15 hours a day. Many special effects technicians work freelance, so there can be long periods of no work (and no pay) between jobs.

Because motion picture scripts often call for filming at various locations, special effects technicians may travel a great deal. Work environments can vary considerably; a technician may remain in a shop or at a computer terminal, or may go on location for a film or television shoot and work outdoors.

OUTLOOK

The competition for jobs in film special effects houses is fierce. For over 20 years now, films of all genres have incorporated computer graphics and high-tech effects, inspiring a whole generation of young people with computers and imaginations. Many of today's top effects professionals credit their love for *Star Wars* with directing them toward careers in the industry. As the cost of powerful computers continues to decrease, even more people will be able to experiment with computer graphics and develop their skills and talents.

Though some special effects companies are very profitable, others are struggling to make enough money to meet their expenses. Production companies are attempting to tighten their budgets and to turn out movies quickly. Therefore, a contract for special effects goes to the lowest bidding effects company. The cost of the effects, including salaries for top technicians, are increasing, while film producers decrease their special effects budgets. This will either be corrected by effects companies demanding more money, or only a few of the very top companies will be able to thrive.

Digital technology will continue to rapidly change the industry. Experts predict that within 10 years, film will be eliminated and movies will be shot and projected digitally, enhancing computer effects. Filmmakers will edit their movies over the Internet. And it may not be long before filmmakers are able to make entire movies with CGI, employing only digital actors. Some companies are experimenting with taking screen images of past and present film stars and digitally creating new films and performances.

FOR MORE INFORMATION

For information about colleges with film and television programs of study, and to read interviews with filmmakers, visit the AFI website.

American Film Institute (AFI)
2021 North Western Avenue
Los Angeles, CA 90027-1657
Tel: 323-856-7600
http://www.afi.com

For extensive information about the digital effects industry, visit the AWN website. The site includes feature articles, a guide to education-related resources, and a career section.

Animation World Network (AWN)
6525 Sunset Boulevard, Garden Suite 10
Los Angeles, CA 90028
Tel: 323-606-4200
Email: info@awn.com
http://www.awn.com

For information on union membership, contact

International Alliance of Theatrical Stage Employees, Moving Picture Technicians, Artists and Allied Crafts of the United States, Its Territories and Canada
1430 Broadway, 20th Floor
New York, NY 10018
Tel: 212-730-1770
http://www.iatse-intl.org

For information about festivals and presentations, and news about the industry, contact
Visual Effects Society
4121 Redwood Avenue, Suite 101
Los Angeles, CA 90066
Tel: 310-822-9181
http://www.visualeffectssociety.com

Cinefex *magazine maintains a helpful list of special effects companies on its website.*
Cinefex
http://www.cinefex.com/index/listings/companies.html

Stunt Performers

OVERVIEW

Stunt performers, also called *stuntmen* and *stuntwomen,* are actors who perform dangerous scenes in motion pictures. They may fall off tall buildings, get knocked from horses and motorcycles, imitate fistfights, and drive in high-speed car chases. They must know how to set up stunts that are both safe to perform and believable to audiences. In these dangerous scenes, stunt performers are often asked to double, or take the place of, a star actor.

HISTORY

There have been stunt performers since the early years of motion pictures. Frank Hanaway, believed to be the first stunt performer, began his career in the 1903 film *The Great Train Robbery.* A former U.S. cavalryman, Hanaway had developed the skill of falling off a horse unharmed. Until the introduction of sound films in the 1920s, stunt performers were used mostly in slapstick comedy films, which relied on sight-gags to entertain the audience.

The first stuntwoman in motion pictures was Helen Gibson, who began her stunt career in the 1914 film series *The Hazards of Helen.* Chosen for the job because of her experience performing tricks on horseback, Gibson went from doubling for Helen Holmes, the star actress, to eventually playing the lead role herself. Among her stunts was jumping from a fast-moving motorcycle onto an adjacent moving locomotive.

Despite the success of Helen Gibson, most stunt performers were men. For dangerous scenes, actresses were usually doubled by a stuntman wearing a wig and the character's costume. Because films

QUICK FACTS

School Subjects
Physical education
Theater/dance

Personal Skills
Following instructions
Mechanical/manipulative

Work Environment
Indoors and outdoors
Primarily multiple locations

Minimum Education Level
High school diploma

Salary Range
$678/day of work to $50,000
to $100,000+

Certification or Licensing
None available

Outlook
About as fast as the average

DOT
159

GOE
N/A

NOC
5232

O*NET-SOC
N/A

usually showed stunts at a distance, audiences could not tell the switch had been made.

Discrimination in the film industry also resulted in few minorities working as stunt performers. White men doubled for American Indians, Asians, Mexicans, and African Americans by applying makeup or other material to their skin. This practice was called "painting down."

As the motion picture industry grew, so did the importance of stunt performers. Because injury to a star actor could end a film project and incur a considerable financial loss for the studio, producers would allow only stunt performers to handle dangerous scenes. Even so, star actors would commonly brag that they had performed their own stunts. Only a few, such as Helen Gibson and Richard Talmadge, actually did.

Beginning in the 1950s the growth in the number of independent, or self-employed, producers brought new opportunities for stunt performers. In general, independent producers were not familiar with stunt work and came to rely on experienced stunt performers to set up stunt scenes and to find qualified individuals to perform them. Stunt performers who did this kind of organizational work came to be called *stunt coordinators*.

The Stuntmen's Association, the first professional organization in the field, was founded in 1960. Its goal was to share knowledge of stunt techniques and safety practices, to work out special problems concerning stunt performers, and to help producers find qualified stunt performers. Other organizations followed, including the International Stunt Association, the Stuntwomen's Association, the United Stuntwomen's Association, Stunts Unlimited, and Drivers Inc. As a result of these organizations, stunt performers are now better educated and trained in stunt techniques.

An increasing number of women and minorities have become stunt performers since the 1970s. The Screen Actors Guild (SAG), the union that represents stunt performers, has been at the vanguard of this change. In the 1970s SAG banned the practice of painting down, thus forcing producers to find, for example, an African-American stuntman to double for an African-American actor. SAG also began to require that producers make an effort to find female stunt performers to double for actresses. Only after showing that a number of qualified stuntwomen have declined the role can a producer hire a stuntman to do the job.

Over the years, new technology has changed the field of stunt work. Air bags, for example, make stunts safer, and faster cars and better brakes have given stunt performers more control. Stunt performers, however, still rely on their athletic ability and sense of timing when doing a dangerous stunt.

THE JOB

Stunt performers work on a wide variety of scenes which have the potential for causing serious injury, including car crashes and chases; fist and sword fights; falls from cars, motorcycles, horses, and buildings; airplane and helicopter gags; rides through river rapids; and confrontations with animals, such as in a buffalo stampede. Although they are hired as actors, they rarely perform a speaking role. Some stunt performers specialize in one type of stunt.

There are two general types of stunt roles: double and nondescript. The first requires a stunt performer to "double"—to take the place of—a star actor in a dangerous scene. As a double, the stunt performer must portray the character in the same way as the star actor. A nondescript role does not involve replacing another person and is usually an incidental character in a dangerous scene. An example of a nondescript role is a driver in a freeway chase scene.

The idea for a stunt usually begins with the screenwriter. Stunts can make a movie not only exciting, but also profitable. Action films, in fact, make up the majority of box-office hits. The stunts, however, must make sense within the context of the film's story.

Once the stunts are written into the script, it is the job of the director to decide how they will appear on the screen. Directors, especially of large, action-filled movies, often seek the help of a stunt coordinator. Stunt coordinators are individuals who have years of experience performing or coordinating stunts and who know the stunt performer community well. A stunt coordinator can quickly determine if a stunt is feasible and, if so, what is the best and safest way to perform it. The stunt coordinator plans the stunt, oversees the setup and construction of special sets and materials, and either hires or recommends the most qualified stunt performer. Some stunt coordinators also take over the direction of action scenes. Because of this responsibility, many stunt coordinators are members not only of the Screen Actors Guild but of the Directors Guild of America.

Although a stunt may last only a few seconds on film, preparations for the stunt can take several hours or even days. Stunt performers work with such departments as props, makeup, wardrobe, and set design. They also work closely with the special effects team to resolve technical problems and ensure safety. The director and the stunt performer must agree on a camera angle that will maximize the effect of the stunt. These preparations can save a considerable amount of production time and money. A carefully planned stunt can often be completed in just one take. More typically, the stunt person will have to perform the stunt several times until the director is satisfied with the performance.

Stunt performers do not have a death wish. They are dedicated professionals who take great precautions to ensure their safety. Air bags, body pads, or cables might be used in a stunt involving a fall or a crash. If a stunt performer must enter a burning building, special fire-proof clothing is worn and protective cream is applied to the skin. Stunt performers commonly design and build their own protective equipment.

Stunt performers are not only actors but also athletes. Thus, they spend much of their time keeping their bodies in top physical shape and practicing their stunts.

REQUIREMENTS

High School

Take physical education, dance, and other courses that will involve you in exercise, weight lifting, and coordination. Sports teams can help you develop the athletic skills needed. In a theater class, you'll learn to take direction, and you may have the opportunity to perform for an audience.

Postsecondary Training

There is no minimum educational requirement for becoming a stunt performer. Most learn their skills by working for years under an experienced stunt performer. A number of stunt schools, however, do exist, including the United Stuntmen's Association National Stunt Training School. You can also benefit from enrolling in theater classes.

Among the skills that must be learned are specific stunt techniques, such as how to throw a punch; the design and building of safety equipment; and production techniques, such as camera angles and film editing. The more a stunt performer knows about all aspects of filmmaking, the better that person can design effective and safe stunts.

Certification or Licensing

There is no certification available, but, like all actors, stunt performers working in film and TV must belong to the Screen Actors Guild (SAG). Many stunt performers also belong to the American Federation of Television and Radio Artists (AFTRA). As a member of a union, you'll receive special benefits, such as better pay and compensation for overtime and holidays.

A stunt performer is helped from his overturned vehicle after the completion of a stunt. *(Rick Doyle, Corbis)*

Other Requirements

Stunt work requires excellent athletic ability. Many stunt performers were high school and college athletes, and some were Olympic or world champions. Qualities developed through sports such as self-discipline, coordination, common sense, and coolness under stress are essential to becoming a successful stunt performer. As a stunt performer, you must exercise regularly to stay in shape and maintain good health. And since you may be working with ropes, cables, and other equipment, you should also have some understanding of the mechanics of the stunts you'll be performing.

Because much of the work involves being a stunt double for a star actor, it is helpful to have a common body type. Exceptionally tall or short people, for example, may have difficulty finding roles.

EXPLORING

There are few means of gaining experience as a stunt performer prior to actual employment. Involvement in high school or college athletics is helpful, as is acting experience in a school or local theater. As an intern or extra for a film production, you may have the opportunity to see stunt people at work. Theme parks and circuses also make much use of stunt performers; some of these places allow visitors to meet the performers after shows.

EMPLOYERS

Most stunt performers work on a freelance basis, contracting with individual productions on a project-by-project basis. Stunt performers working on TV projects may have long-term commitments if serving as a stand-in for a regular character. Some stunt performers also work in other aspects of the entertainment industry, taking jobs with theme parks, and live stage shows and events.

STARTING OUT

Most stunt performers enter the field by contacting stunt coordinators and asking for work. Coordinators and stunt associations can be located in trade publications. To be of interest to coordinators, you'll need to promote any special skills you have, such as stunt driving, skiing, and diving. Many stunt performers also have agents who locate work for them, but an agent can be very difficult to get if you have no stunt experience. If you live in New York or Los Angeles, you should volunteer to work as an intern for an action film; you may have the chance to meet some of the stunt performers, and make connections with crew members and other industry professionals. You can also submit a resume to the various online services, such as StuntNET (http://www.stunt-net.com), that are used by coordinators and casting directors. If you attend a stunt school, you may develop important contacts in the field.

ADVANCEMENT

New stunt performers generally start with simple roles, such as being one of 40 people in a brawl scene. With greater experience and training, stunt performers can get more complicated roles. Some stunt associations have facilities where stunt performers work out and practice their skills. After a great deal of experience, you may be invited to join a professional association such as the Stuntmen's Association of Motion Pictures, which will allow you to network with others in the industry.

About five to 10 years of experience are usually necessary to become a stunt coordinator. Some stunt coordinators eventually work as a director of action scenes.

EARNINGS

The earnings of stunt performers vary considerably by their experience and the difficulty of the stunts they perform. In 2005, the minimum daily salary of stunt performers and coordinators in the motion picture and television industries was $716. Stunt performers and coordinators working on a weekly basis in either motion pictures or television earned a minimum of $2,666 per week. Though this may seem like a lot of money, few stunt performers work every day. According to the SAG, the majority of its 120,000 members make less than $7,500. But those who are in high demand can receive salaries of well over $100,000 a year.

Stunt performers usually negotiate their salaries with the stunt coordinator. In general, they are paid per stunt; if they have to repeat the stunt three times before the director likes the scene, the stunt performer gets paid three times. If footage of a stunt is used in another film, the performer is paid again. The more elaborate and dangerous the stunt, the more money the stunt performer receives. Stunt performers are also compensated for overtime and travel expenses. Stunt coordinators negotiate their salaries with the producer.

WORK ENVIRONMENT

The working conditions of a stunt performer change from project to project. It could be a studio set, a river, or an airplane thousands of feet above the ground. Like all actors, they are given their own dressing rooms.

Careers in stunt work tend to be short. The small number of jobs is one reason, as are age and injury. Even with the emphasis on safety, injuries commonly occur, often because of mechanical failure, problems with animals, or human error. The possibility of death is always present. Despite these drawbacks, a large number of people are attracted to the work because of the thrill, the competitive challenge, and the chance to work in motion pictures.

OUTLOOK

There are over 2,500 stunt performers who belong to SAG, but only a fraction of those can afford to devote themselves to film work full time. Stunt coordinators will continue to hire only very experienced professionals, making it difficult to break into the business.

The future of the profession may be affected by computer technology. In more cases, filmmakers may choose to use special effects and computer-generated imagery for action sequences. Not only can computer effects allow for more ambitious images, but they're also safer. Safety on film sets has always been a serious concern; despite innovations in filming techniques, stunts remain very dangerous. However, using live stunt performers can give a scene more authenticity, so talented stunt performers will always be in demand.

FOR MORE INFORMATION

For information on salaries, benefits, and latest industry news, visit
Screen Actors Guild
5757 Wilshire Boulevard
Los Angeles, CA 90036-3600
Tel: 323-954-1600
http://www.sag.com

For information on opportunities in the industry, contact the following organizations
Stuntmen's Association of Motion Pictures
10660 Riverside Drive, 2nd Floor, Suite E
Toluca Lake, CA 91602
Tel: 818-766 4334
Email: info@stuntmen.com
http://www.stuntmen.com

Stuntwomen's Association of Motion Pictures
Tel: 818-762-0907
Email: stuntwomen@stuntwomen.com
http://www.stuntwomen.com

For information about the USA training program, contact
United Stuntmen's Association
10924 Mukilteo Speedway, PMB 272
Mukilteo, WA 98275
Tel: 425-290-9957
Email: bushman4@prodigy.net
http://www.stuntschool.com

Talent Agents and Scouts

OVERVIEW

An agent is a salesperson who sells artistic or athletic talent. *Talent agents* act as representatives for actors, directors, writers, models, athletes, and other people who work in the arts, advertising, sports, and fashion. (This article focuses primarily on agents in film and television.) Agents promote their clients' talent and manage their legal contractual business.

HISTORY

The wide variety of careers that exists in the film and television industries today evolved gradually. In the 19th century in England and America, leading actors and actresses developed a system, called the "actor-manager system," in which the actor both performed and handled business and financial arrangements. Over the course of the 20th century, responsibilities diversified. In the first decades of the century, major studios took charge of the actors' professional and financial management.

In the 1950s the major studio monopolies were broken, and control of actors and contracts came up for grabs. Resourceful business-minded people became agents when they realized that there was money to be made by controlling access to the talent behind movie and television productions. They became middlemen between actors (and other creative people) and the production studios, charging commissions for use of their clients.

Currently, commissions range between 10 and 15 percent of the money an actor earns in a production. In more recent years, agents have formed revolutionary deals for their stars, making more money for agencies and actors alike. Powerful agencies such as Creative Artists Agency, International Creative Management, and the William Morris Agency are credited with (or, by some, accused of) heralding in the age of the multimillion-dollar deal for film stars. This has proved controversial, as some top actor fees have inflated to over $20 million per picture; some industry professionals worry that high actor salaries are cutting too deeply into film budgets, while others believe that actors are finally getting their fair share of the profits. Whichever the case, the film industry still thrives, and filmmakers still compete for the highest priced talent. And the agent, always an active player in the industry, has become even more influential in how films are made.

THE JOB

Talent agents act as representatives for actors, writers, and others who work in the entertainment industry. They look for clients who have potential for success and then work aggressively to promote their clients to film and television directors, casting directors, production companies, advertising companies, and other potential employers. Agents work closely with clients to find assignments that will best achieve clients' career goals.

Agents find clients in several ways. Those who work for an agency might be assigned a client by the agency, based on experience or a compatible personality. Some agents also work as *talent scouts* and actively search for new clients, whom they then bring to an agency. Or the clients themselves might approach agents who have good reputations and request their representation. Agents involved in the film and television industries review portfolios, screen tests, and audiotapes to evaluate potential clients' appearance, voice, personality, experience, ability to take direction, and other factors.

When an agent agrees to represent a client, they both sign a contract that specifies the extent of representation, the time period, payment, and other legal considerations.

When agents look for jobs for their clients, they do not necessarily try to find as many assignments as possible. Agents try to carefully choose assignments that will further their clients' careers. For example, an agent might represent an actor who wants to work in film, but is having difficulty finding a role. The agent looks for roles in commercials, music videos, or voice-overs that will give the actor some exposure.

Agents also work closely with the potential employers of their clients. They need to satisfy the requirements of both parties. Agents who represent actors have a network of directors, producers, advertising executives, and photographers that they contact frequently to see if any of their clients can meet their needs.

When agents see a possible match between employer and client, they speak to both and quickly organize meetings, interviews, or auditions so that employers can meet potential hires and evaluate their work and capabilities. Agents must be persistent and aggressive on behalf of their clients. They spend time on the phone with employers, convincing them of their clients' talents and persuading them to hire clients. There may be one or several interviews, and the agent may coach clients through this process to make sure clients understand what the employer is looking for and adapt their presentations accordingly. When a client achieves success and is in great demand, the agent receives calls, scripts, and other types of work requests and passes along only those that are appropriate to the interests and goals of the client.

When an employer agrees to hire a client, the agent helps negotiate a contract that outlines salary, benefits, promotional appearances, and other fees, rights, and obligations. Agents have to look out for the best interests of their clients and at the same time satisfy employers in order to establish continuing, longlasting relationships.

In addition to promoting individuals, agents may also work to make package deals—for example, combining a writer, director, and a star to make up a package, which they then market to production studios. The agent charges a packaging commission to the studio in addition to the commissions agreed to in each package member's contract. A strong package can be very lucrative for the agency or agencies who represent the talent involved, since the package commission is often a percentage of the total budget of the production.

Agents often develop lifelong working relationships with their clients. They act as business associates, advisers, advocates, mentors, teachers, guardians, and confidantes. Because of the complicated nature of these relationships, they can be volatile, so a successful relationship requires trust and respect on both sides, which can only be earned through experience and time. Agents who represent high-profile talent make up only a small percentage of agency work. Most agents represent lesser-known or locally known talent.

The largest agencies are located in Los Angeles and New York, where film, theater, advertising, publishing, fashion, and art-buying industries are centered. There are modeling and theatrical agencies in most large cities, however, and independent agents are established throughout the country.

REQUIREMENTS

High School

You should take courses in business, mathematics, and accounting to prepare for the management aspects of an agent's job. Take English and speech courses to develop good communication skills because an agent must be gifted at negotiation. You also need a good eye for talent, so you need to develop some expertise in film, theater, art, literature, advertising, sports, or whatever field you hope to specialize in.

Postsecondary Training

There are no formal requirements for becoming an agent, but a bachelor's degree is strongly recommended. Advanced degrees in law and business are becoming increasingly prevalent; law and business training are useful because agents are responsible for writing contracts according to legal regulations. However, in some cases an agent may obtain this training on the job. Agents come from a variety of backgrounds; some of them have worked as actors and then shifted into agent careers because they enjoyed working in the industry. Agents who have degrees from law or business schools have an advantage when it comes to advancing their careers or opening a new agency.

Other Requirements

It is most important to be willing to work hard and aggressively pursue opportunities for clients. You should be detail-oriented and have a good head for business; contract work requires meticulous attention to detail. You need a great deal of self-motivation and ambition to develop good contacts in industries that may be difficult to break into. You should be comfortable talking with all kinds of people and be able to develop relationships easily. It helps to be a good general conversationalist in addition to being knowledgeable about your field.

EXPLORING

To learn more about working as an agent in the film and television industries, read publications agents read, such as *Variety* (http://www.variety.com), *The Hollywood Reporter* (http://www.hollywoodreporter.com), *Premiere* (http://www.premiere.com), and *Entertainment Weekly* (http://www.ew.com). See current movies to get a sense of the established and up-and-coming talents in the film industry. Trace the careers of actors you like, including their early work in independent films, commercials, and stage work.

If you live in Los Angeles or New York, you may be able to volunteer or intern at an agency to find out more about the career. If you live outside Los Angeles and New York, check your phone book's Yellow Pages, or search the Web, for listings of local agencies. Most major cities have agents who represent local performing artists, actors, and models. If you contact them, they may be willing to offer you some insight into the nature of talent management in general.

EMPLOYERS

Talent agencies are located all across the United States, handling a variety of talents. Those agencies that represent artists and professionals in the film industry are located primarily in Los Angeles. Some film agencies, such as the William Morris Agency, are located in New York. An agency may specialize in a particular type of talent, such as minority actors, extras, or TV commercial actors. The top three film agencies—Creative Artists Agency, International Creative Management, and the William Morris Agency—employ approximately 1,500 agents.

STARTING OUT

The best way to enter this field is to seek an internship with an agency. If you live in or can spend a summer in Los Angeles or New York, you have an advantage in terms of numbers of opportunities. Libraries and bookstores will have resources for locating talent agencies. By searching the Web, you can find many free listings of reputable agents. The Screen Actors Guild also maintains a list of franchised agents that is available on its website. The Yellow Pages will yield a list of local talent agencies. For those who live in Los Angeles, there are employment agencies that deal specifically with talent agent careers. Compile a list of agencies that may offer internship opportunities. Some internships will be paid and others may provide college course credit, but most importantly, they will provide you with experience and contacts in the industry. An intern who works hard and knows something about the business stands a good chance of securing an entry-level position at an agency. At the top agencies, this will be a position in the mail room, where almost everyone starts. In smaller agencies, it may be an assistant position. Eventually persistence, hard work, and cultivated connections will lead to a job as an agent.

ADVANCEMENT

Once you have a job as an assistant, you will be allowed to work closely with an agent to learn the ropes. You may be able to read contracts and listen in on phone calls and meetings. You will begin to take on some of your own clients as you gain experience. Agents who wish to advance must work aggressively on behalf of their clients as well as seek out quality talent to bring into an agency. Those who are successful command more lucrative salaries and may choose to open their own agencies. Some agents find that their work is a good stepping stone toward a different career in the industry.

EARNINGS

Earnings for agents vary greatly, depending on the success of the agent and his or her clients. An agency receives 10 to 15 percent of a client's fee for a project. An agent is then paid a commission by the agency as well as a base salary. According to the U.S. Department of Labor, agents and business managers who were employed in the motion picture and video industries earned a mean annual salary of $81,110 in 2004. Salaries for agents and business managers employed in all industries ranged from less than $25,630 to more than $121,710 annually.

Working for an agency, an experienced agent will receive health and retirement benefits, bonuses, and paid travel and accommodations.

WORK ENVIRONMENT

Work in a talent agency can be lively and exciting. It is rewarding to watch a client attain success with your help. The work can seem very glamorous, allowing you to rub elbows with the rich and famous and make contacts with the most powerful people in the entertainment industry. Most agents, however, represent less famous actors, directors, and other industry professionals.

Agents' work requires a great deal of stamina and determination in the face of setbacks. The work can be extremely stressful, even in small agencies. It often demands long hours, including evenings and weekends. To stay successful, agents at the top of the industry must constantly network. They spend a great deal of time on the telephone, with both clients and others in the industry, and attending industry functions.

OUTLOOK

Employment in the arts and entertainment field is expected to grow rapidly in response to the demand for entertainment from a growing population. However, the numbers of artists and performers also continues to grow, creating fierce competition for all jobs in this industry. This competition will drive the need for more agents and scouts to find talented individuals and place them in the best jobs.

Despite a plethora of entertainment options available today, the American public retains a strong love of movies—whether viewed in theatres or at home. With markets overseas expanding, even the films that don't do so well domestically can still turn a tidy profit. As a result, agents at all levels in the film industry will continue to thrive. Also, more original cable television programming will lead to more actors and performers seeking representation.

FOR MORE INFORMATION

Visit the SAG website for information about acting in films and for a list of talent agencies.

Screen Actors Guild (SAG)
5757 Wilshire Boulevard
Los Angeles, CA 90036-3600
Tel: 323-954-1600
http://www.sag.com

Index